What It Means to Be Jewish

INA ABRAMS

WHAT IT
MEANS TO BE
JEWISH

The Voices of Our Heritage

ST. MARTIN'S PRESS ❧ NEW YORK

www.stmartins.com

Permissions begin on page 226.

ISBN 0-312-26194-2

First Edition: June 2002

10 9 8 7 6 5 4 3 2 1

To the memory of my parents,
Betty and Leopold Schwartz,
and of
Benjamin Golub

Contents

Acknowledgments

I am forever indebted to Joan Golub for bringing me her father's book, which ultimately became the cornerstone for this one. Barry Friedman, close friend first, then rabbi, encouraged my newfound love of Judaism and treated it with respect and care. Throughout the preparation of this book, he has been an adviser, teacher, spiritual guide, and touchstone. I will always be grateful for his continuing support.

Thanks are also due to Laura Yorke, then editor at Golden Books, who guided this project with unending sagacity and enthusiasm during its initial stages. Subsequently, Lara Asher took it over and helped me refine the manuscript as I completed the work. I thank her for her keen perceptiveness, dedication, and for coming up with the perfect title. For their excellent comments after reading, and rereading, various parts of this book, I am deeply grateful to Leslie Garfield and Suze Schwartz. Kim Witherspoon continues to be the best agent an author could ask for.

For influencing me personally by the Jewish lives they lead, I must mention Leslie Garfield, Liora Yalof, Miriam Ruzow, Shula Reinharz, Elaine and Elie Housman, Alan Jacobs, and my old and precious friend Galia Golan.

Unbounding gratitude for the generosity of three strangers, all rabbis, who agreed to read and comment on this manuscript in its early stages. Their criticism and notations, provided in meticulous detail, were not only invaluable but were, in fact, also an education in themselves. I am eternally grateful to Rabbi Rifat Sonsino, of Temple Beth Shalom in Needham,

Massachusetts; to Rabbi Lisa Hochberg-Miller of Temple Israel in Long Beach, California; and most especially to Rabbi Alan Fuchs, Rabbi Emeritus of Congregation Rodeph Shalom in Philadelphia, who has since become both mentor and dear friend.

Rabbi Alexander Schindler was most gracious in agreeing to write the foreword for this book. His life has inspired more than three generations of Jews, including this author. His untimely death leaves a void in more people than he will ever know.

Many writers conclude their acknowledgments by thanking their spouses for reading, editing and commenting on their manuscripts. My husband, Herbert Yalof, did none of the above. He did, however, listen to the idea in its larval stage, replied, "Sounds great to me," and will read it for the first time along with the rest of you—which is just how I wanted it. Thanks, Herb.

FOREWORD

In the course of my rabbinical career, which now spans forty years, I must have given well over three thousand speeches, sermons, invocations, and formal addresses. I traversed this continent from coast to coast and north to south, speaking to congregational and community groups. These visits always left a trail of Jewish aphorisms. Invariably, I brought at least one book of quotations along with me, in the hope that browsing through its pages en route I would find still another nugget, another passage expressing a mood about the human and the divine, that would illuminate and dramatize my message. Unfortunately, I did not have this splendid anthology by Ina Abrams.

In general, anthologies are a source of delight for their readers. But they also serve a far greater purpose: they are an indispensable reference guide for scholars and teachers and preachers whose writings would be dry as dust when unadorned by the wise and often witty words these very special books have to offer.

What It Means to Be Jewish is more than an anthology, however. It is a book of *inclusion*. First, because Ms. Abrams makes the invaluable treasures of Jewish scripture, literature, and history accessible even to the nascent reader of Judaica. And second, because the *structure* of the book offers both Jews and non-Jews a sense of the cultural and spiritual evolution of Judaism and the Jewish identity. To this end, the book takes us on a journey from biblical times to today, intertwining the words of Hillel and Louis Brandeis, Mark

Twain and Winston Churchill, Martin Buber and Philip Roth, Golda Meir and Yitzhak Rabin into a multicolored tapestry of literary and ethnic diversity that reflects the rich and universal texture of Jewish living and Jewish life.

Ms. Abrams's book is inclusive in another significant way: among the insights she includes of contemporary sages, those of women are most notable. To see Letty Cottin Pogrebin and Nina Beth Cardin, Blu Greenberg and Sue Levi Elwell, Justice Ruth Bader Ginsburg and Cynthia Ozick, Rachel Alder and Laura Geller all present with the "usual cast of characters" in a Jewish anthology is to see the unfolding reality of Judaism, which has been enlarged and transformed by the creative intervention of these and many other Jewish women. Ina Abrams's perceptive editorial eye succeeds in capturing the very essence of that transformation and distilling it for our study and use.

To the modern Jew, the Torah has not only been a completed and codified teaching, but also an ongoing revelation that each generation must experience and interpret. To do so, each generation must have its scholars and rabbis, willing and capable of journeying deeply into the garden of Judaism. Of no less significance, however, are the popularizers of each generation, who collect the seeds from that garden and sow them far and wide, in the hope of capturing the hearts of those Jews who merely pause to "smell the roses."

Ina Abrams has done so, producing, in this anthology, an exquisite and captivating bouquet.

—RABBI ALEXANDER M. SCHINDLER

GLOSSARY

Adon Olom. Eternal Lord. Morning service prayer, often chanted at conclusion of the Sabbath and at festival services.

afikoman. Matzo hidden before the Passover meal to be found and redeemed for a prize later.

Ahm Israel. People of Israel.

al pilkiddush haShem. For the sanctification of God's name.

Alenu. Adoration.

aliyah, aliyot. The honor of being called to the Torah to recite blessings before and after the Torah is read during services. Also means "immigration to Israel."

babushka. Russian grandmother.

bar mitzvah. Popularly translated as "son/daughter of the commandments." For a boy, this happens at age thirteen, for a girl (bas mitzvah or bat mitzvah) it's twelve and a day.

Beit Ha-Midrash. Synagogue.

Bet Ha-Knesset. The House of Assembly.

Bet Ha-Midrash. The House of Study.

Bet Ha-Tfillah. The House of Prayer.

Birhot Ha-Shahar. Morning blessings.

Brith Milah, brith, brit, bris. Circumcision ritual by which an eight-day-old boy enters the Covenant of Abraham. The word *brith* means "covenant."

bubbe. Grandmother.

cabala, cabbala, cabbalah, kabala, kabbala, kabbalah. The texts comprising the Jewish mystical tradition.

Chalutzim. Pioneers of the early Israel.

Cohen. A tribe of priests from the early days of the first temple.

daven. Pray.

dreidel, dredl. A four-sided top with Hebrew letters, traditionally played at Passover.

Eretz Israel. The Jewish homeland.

gedakhte. Thick.

geirim. Proselytes, or people who convert to Judaism.

gelt. Coins usually given out to children as gifts at Hanukkah.

ger tzedek. Righteous proselyte.

goy. Non-Jew (Plural: goyim.)

hakafot. Torah procession whereby the Torah is carried around the synagogue.

halakah. Body of Jewish law, especially the legal part of the Talmud.

Hanukkah, Chanukah. Festival of Lights. Jewish holiday that marks the victory of the Maccabees over the Assyrian Greeks, and the liberation and rededication of the Temple in Jerusalem to the worship of God.

heder. Elementary Jewish school that teaches children to read the Torah and other scripture in Hebrew.

hitpallel. To judge oneself.

kaddish. An ancient Aramaic mourner's prayer that is recited during synagogue services, an expression of the mourner's faith that even in periods of deep sadness, he still believes in God and life itself. This prayer for the dead is usually recited in a minyan.

kibbutz. An agricultural farm of the kind started in the 1900s with a socialist philosophy. (Plural: kibbutzim.)

kibbutznik. Kibbutz worker.

Kristallnacht. "The night of broken glass." A seminal event of the Holocaust.

Ladino. A combination of the Spanish and Hebrew languages.

latke. Potato pancake, a traditional Hanukkah treat.

Levi. A tribe of priests from the early days of the first temple.

Ma'ariv. Weekday evening service.

mehitzah. A partition for separating men and women so they cannot see each other, used in many Orthodox synagogues.

melamed. Teacher.

mezuzah, mezuza. A piece of parchment inscribed with a verse from the Bible that is rolled up and placed in a case and attached to the doorpost of a house, as annotated in Deuteronomy 6:9— "And you shalt write them [the commandments] on the doorposts of thy house. . . ."

mikdash ma'at. A little sanctuary—said of a Jewish home.

mikveh. A bath in ritual waters taken prior to conversion to Judaism, represents spiritual purification.

Minhah. Afternoon prayers.

minyan. A quorum of ten people required for morning and evening prayer service.

mitzvah. A good deed, a divine command. (Plural: mitzvoth, mitzvot.)

Moabites. Persons descending from Moab, a country in ancient Israel.

mohel. The person who performs a circumcision of a baby boy.

oberscharfuhrer. German officer.

pallal. To judge.

Passover, Pesach. Jewish holiday commemorating the liberation from slavery in Egypt, festival of spring.

Purim. Celebration of the deliverance of the Persian Jews from Prime Minister Haman.

pushke. Small receptacle for coins that are later given to Jewish charity.

rabbi, rebbe. Teacher, official leader of Jewish congregation.

reboyne sheloylem. The Almighty.

Rosh Hashanah. The beginning of the Jewish New Year.

seder. The traditional Passover meal, generally held the first and second nights of Passover.

Shabbat. Hebrew word for Sabbath or Saturday.

shalom. Peace, hello, goodbye.

Shavuot. Jewish holiday marking the harvest of the first fruits.

Sheerit ha-Pelatah. "The remnant that was saved."

Shekhinah. A cabalist term usually (but not always) feminine by fact or association. Describes the chief object of both the divine and human search for wholeness and perfection.

Shema. Delaration of faith.

shivah. *Shivah* means "seven," and it is the name given to the traditional seven days of mourning. Sitting shivah is the practice of receiving guests generally at the home of the deceased to join in a seven-day mourning period after a death. Shivah is not observed on the Sabbath.

shofar. Ram's horn traditionally blown on Rosh Hashanah to signal the entry of the New Year. Also sounded at the end of Yom Kippur.

shtetl. Small Eastern European Jewish town or village.

shul. Synagogue.

siddur. Jewish prayer book. (Plural: siddurim.)

Simchat Torah, Simchas Torah. Festival celebrating the completion of the reading of the Torah, "rejoicing in the Torah."

Sukkoth, Sukkot. Festival of booths, falls five days after Yom Kippur.

t'phila, t'fillah. Prayer.

tallith, tallis, or tallit. Prayer shawl.

tante. Aunt.

ten lanu shalom. Give us peace.

teshuva. Repentance.

tikkun olam. A central concept of Judaism, which means to correct the world's ills, repair the world, make it a better place for all to live.

tsimes. Traditional baked dish of carrots, potatoes, and raisins.

tzedakah. Charity.

yahrzeit. The anniversary of a Jewish person's death.

Yiddish. A combination of the German and Hebrew languages.

Yom Kippur. Jewish holiday, also called Day of Atonement.

zaddik, tzadik. Righteous or holy person. (Plural: zaddikim.)

Zay gezunt. Be well.

INTRODUCTION

Several years ago, for no reason that I can explain, I began a renewal of my life as a Jew. Suddenly I found myself wrestling with a whole series of questions—about the origins and character of my heritage and the gifts that it offers, about a Jew's obligation as one of the "chosen" people, about Zionism and its relationship to religion. How did *practicing* Jews see the world, I wondered. Was it different from the way *I* saw it?

My search for answers led me to the best sources I could find. Books, rabbis, and teachers became my guides. Aware of my growing interest, one day a friend presented me with a cherished possession. It was a well-worn, palm-size book entitled *A Book of Jewish Thoughts*, which had, at one time, belonged to her father. It anthologized writings assembled by England's chief rabbi, Dr. Joseph H. Hertz. Originally published in England in 1917, a 1925 edition of the book was distributed by the American Jewish Welfare board to 160,000 American servicemen. During World War II, many of our soldiers and sailors—perhaps my friend's father among them—carried it in the back pockets of their uniforms throughout battle-torn Europe.

The passages in the book illuminated all the richness of the Jewish experience, describing in one relevant selection after another what it means to be a Jew. Here were the words of Solomon Schechter, theologian and essayist of the 1800s and Emma Lazarus, whose poem, the "New Colossus," is inscribed on the base of the Statue of Liberty. Here, too, were

Theodor Herzl, the father of the political Zionist movement, and Stephen Wise, the great American rabbi of his time. But glaringly absent were some of the most gifted writers and creative thinkers of *our* day—Isaac Bashevis Singer, Saul Bellow, and Abraham Joshua Heschel, to name a few. There was a Yiddish Cradle Song from 1892 but no "Wedding Song" from the 1962 musical *Fiddler on the Roof*. And, of course, no reference to the Holocaust or the State of Israel. How could there be when these two watershed events of modern Jewish history had not yet occurred?

The book was near perfection in capturing the spiritual and cultural aspects of Judaism, but its abrupt ending in 1923 left me longing for an updated version. Aware of the magnitude of my task, I chose to create that version myself.

From the beginning, I did not know where my research would take me or what my ultimate destination would be. Some days were spent perusing the stacks in the Boston Public Library, tracking down obscure, dusty volumes that had been tucked away and forgotten. Other days I would sit for hours in the Dorit Jewish Division at the New York Public Library, mesmerized by both the ancient and contemporary books of Jewish lore. Widener Library at Harvard opened its stacks to me, and, with great reverence, I meandered among the shelves of centuries-old books, removing with great care the aged volumes. One afternoon, late, I searched for the prayer I recited at my confirmation, but I never found it. I did, however, find a poem by Emma Lazarus that I had memorized as a child.

As exhilarating as the research was, deciding what should be included in the book became an overwhelming task. While the pieces in Rabbi Hertz's book had initially inspired me, I chose to repeat very few of them as I uncovered selections I considered more reflective of Judaism and its place in the modern world.

I set certain parameters for my choices. For example,

whenever possible, I selected first-person writings in an effort to allow the people who experienced the events to describe them in their own words: a young writer attends his first Hasidic wedding in Brooklyn; a child poetically reflects on the "last butterfly" as it flies over the wall of his ghetto at Therezinstadt. Amos Oz describes his father on the night the United Nations declared Israel an independent state:

> About two o'clock in the morning, my father brought me back home and put me to bed. Then he climbed in beside me, still in his clothes—something he never did. In the pitch dark, he told me stories of how he'd been abused by anti-Semites back in Vilna in his youth. . . . I remember him explaining to me that I might still be bullied in school, but not for being Jewish. This was the significance of the Jewish state. And I saw— well, I didn't really see, because it was so dark—but rather I sensed tears on his face. It was the first and probably the only time I saw my father cry.

When male and female authors wrote equally well on the same topic, I usually gave preference to the women's writings, particularly from the early years. That is because until the seventies, when the Jewish feminist movement took shape, women's voices in writings and scholarship were often too gentle to be heard.

This book is meant to define the Jewish experience through the ages. It represents a spectrum of concerns of the Jewish people from the secular to the spiritual. Some passages capture the essence of Jewish thought and the inexplicable connection that all Jewish people—no matter where they are from—seem to have with one another. Still others reflect the ways Jews have been seen and identified by the world, and how they see themselves.

Overall, *What It Means to Be Jewish* is designed to be accessible to a wide audience. It speaks to both the religious *and* the nonpracticing Jew; it is for the newest generation of immigrants as well as for Christians looking for a better understanding of their neighbors. I tried to be as comprehensive as possible in my selections, but there may be places a reader will wish had been expanded.

Chapter 1, "To Be a Jew," delves into the hearts and minds of the Jewish people as they report on their covenant with God and their own sense of identity. Contained here are some of the most enduring ideas professed by Jewish luminaries throughout the ages.

The second chapter, "It's a Tradition!," illuminates significant components of Jewish life. Jews have always transmitted their heritage through the celebration of holidays and the telling and retelling of stories. This segment provides an overview of rituals, lore, and customs associated with the life cycle and the Jewish calendar. Other defining aspects of Jewish culture, such as Jewish humor and the role of women in Judaism, round out the chapter.

The next two chapters follow the amazing forward march of the Jews of the nineteenth and twentieth centuries. "Coming to America" recounts the dramatic experiences of Jewish immigrants who crossed the Atlantic in search of the promise of the New World. The story begins in the Russian shtetl, shifts abruptly to the horrors of the pogroms, and continues on to the stifling lower deck of a ship as it steams across the Atlantic toward the "Promised Land." After two weeks crossing with her whole family, a woman sits with her small daughter on a bench in the immigration center at Ellis Island pondering a dilemma: The ill child has been denied entry to America. Should the entire family return to the Old Country? Or should some members stay behind? We learn of the hardships faced by the first generation of American Jewish immigrants, but also of the joys of life in this country as writers such as Philip Roth and Paul Cowan offer us a vivid glimpse of what it was like, as children and grandchildren of immigrants, growing up Jewish in America.

Between June 1941 and May 1945, six million Jews perished at the hands of the Nazis and their collaborators. In "We Remember the Six Million," writings of the Holocaust include the words of well-known authors such as Elie Wiesel and Lucy Dawidowicz, and of the many more who will forever remain anonymous, even as their words survived the ghettos, the work camps, and the death marches. With each passage it becomes clearer that "six million" is only a faceless number. "The holocaust" as Judith Miller writes, was achingly "one by one by one . . ."

"Toward the Land of Milk and Honey" covers the span of Jewish history from the birth of the Zionist movement through the creation of the Jewish state in Palestine to be called Israel. From Theodor Herzl's motivating words—"If you will it, it is no dream"—to Prime Minister Yitzhak Rabin's plea for peace just minutes before he was assassinated by a radical Jew, we hear the voices of civilians, soldiers, and notable dignitaries who were behind the founding of the State of Israel and continue today in the unending quest for peace in the Middle East.

Sometimes our cause is advanced by sources other than our own. "As Others See Us" is a testament to the Jewish people by non-Jews. This section includes excerpts from books, journalistic writings, letters, and speeches. Dmitry Shostakovich, the Russian composer, tells of waiting twenty-five years to hear his violin concerto, *The Jewish Cycle*, performed in public. The distinguished *New York Times* editor Harrison Salisbury, chronicles how it feels to be young—and Christian—growing up in a Jewish neighborhood in New York. Mark Twain poetically questions the secret of the Jews' immortality.

"Paths of Prayer" and "Words of Wisdom" are the final two

chapters of the book. The prayers include excerpts from the Holy Scriptures as well as from the siddur, the Jewish prayer book, some of which are old and familiar, some of more recent composition. I have included several of my own favorites, particularly a prayer for peace that I hope will one day be unnecessary. "Words of Wisdom" showcases the voices of both contemporary Jews and of our Jewish sages—Hillel the Elder, Rabbi Akiba, Moses Maimonides, the Ba'al Shem Tov, and Nachman of Bratslav. Political, ethical, and moral guides to living are described in passages from the Talmud, Moses Maimonides' twelfth-century legal code the *Mishne Torah*, the mystical writings of the kabala, and the tomes of the Hasidic masters.

Eventually, an artist must lay down his brush and call it "a painting." The hard part for me was to put an end to my formal research and call it "a manuscript." I did this several months ago, but I have not stopped reading books on Judaism. There is still so much to learn.

Last week, I came across a volume, *From the Fair*, the autobiography of Shalom Aleichem. The dedication, to his "beloved children," so closely expresses my sentiments, I have chosen to include it here. He wrote,

> I know that my book, like any man's work, is not free of defects, but . . . I've given it the best of what I have—my *heart*. Read it from time to time. Perhaps you or your children will learn something from it—how to love our people and appreciate their spiritual treasures that lie scattered in all the dark corners of the vast Diaspora in this large world. . . .

This book is for *my* children and my grandchildren, those whom I know and those not yet born. I hope that as contemporary Jews, they—and indeed all children—will celebrate the richness of their heritage alongside the joys of modern-day Judaism. May the wisdom in this volume be a cherished extension of their learning.

— INA ABRAMS

ONE

TO BE A JEW

Ours is not an I-Thou religion; ours is a We-Thou religion. To be a Jew means to be a cousin of the Jew in Cairo and the Jew in Calcutta, the Jew in Berlin and the Jew in Baghdad, the Jew in New York and the Jew in New Delhi. To be a Jew means to be connected, horizontally and vertically, to all the Jews around the world and to all the Jews of the past, the present, and the future. To be a Jew means to be a great-great-great-great grandchild of Abraham our father and to be a great-great-great-great ancestor of the Messiah. We come before God not by our own merits but as part of a people. A Jew by himself is impossible.

RABBI JACK REIMER

If you are lost in a strange town, find the Jews. Jews will always take care of their own.

BONNIE ZIMMERMAN

FOR MILLENNIA, SAGES and scholars and everyday Jews have tried to define the Jewish identity. It is a question that remains indefinable, even to contemporary Jews. Is one Jewish because he or she goes to synagogue, joins Hadassah, donates to the United Jewish Appeal? Are we Jews because we accept Judaism? Because there is a drop of Jewish blood in our veins? The most enduring definition of the Jewish identity has been that found in the *halakah*, which tells us only those who are born to a Jewish mother or have converted to Judaism can be considered Jews. (Members of the Reform Movement are challenging this law on a very grand scale.)

In modern times, the pursuit for definition of the Jewish identity has become even more difficult. Law and communal responsibility, shared history and culture are all ingredients to defining the Jews. The Hebrew language, central to Jewish prayer, Yiddish, and Ladino have all contributed not only a literature and music but also a culture that enriches all Jewish life. Also central to the definition, purpose, and meaning of Judaism is the concept of *tikkun olam*, correcting the ills that afflict the world. The observance of the mitzvah is not something dependent upon an individual's whim or momentary desire. It is a divine command, which may explain the presence of Jews in so many endeavors devoted to the public well being.

While identity in the greater sense is referent to individualism, for the Jew it calls to mind the way that Jews, no matter the circumstances, have always been linked together. There is a two-thousand-year-old legend that tells of two men sitting in a rowboat. One is amazed to suddenly find water pouring into the boat. He discovers his friend drilling a hole into the floor of the boat and shouts, "What are you doing? Look at the water! We'll sink and drown!" His friend answers, "Don't worry, the hole is under my seat." That ancient maxim teaches that we may not separate ourselves from the community. As we share in its blessings, so we bear the responsibility to contribute to and further those blessings to the benefit of all.

When I began writing this book, I was uncertain of my own Jewish identity. I knew only that I was a returning Jew. But somewhere along the way I stopped returning and now consider myself "returned." Still, after two years at this labor, I continue to define myself as a seeker; I continue to sit at the feet of the sages and rabbis, the living and the dead. Working on this manuscript has greatly illuminated my path. It has opened me to the part of Jewish culture that gives texture to my life: Jewish history, Jewish literature, and yes, even Jewish neurosis. And it has shown me how I, too, am connected; I am such a small part of a continuum that began with Abraham and Sarah, continued through Joseph, Moses and Miriam, Isaiah, King David, Ruth and Esther, Hillel and Moses Maimonides and Martin Buber, Golda Meir and Felix Frankfurter and Jonas Salk, and Barbra Streisand and me. But I *am* a part of it.

In short, I *know* I am a Jew. And in the end, that's all that matters, isn't it?

*   *   *

I AM A JEW

I am a Jew because, born of Israel and having lost her, I
have felt her live again in me, more living than myself.
I am a Jew because the faith of Israel demands of me no
abdication of the mind.
I am a Jew because the faith of Israel requires of me all the
devotion of my heart.
I am a Jew because in every place where suffering exists, the
Jew weeps.
I am a Jew because at every time when despair cries out, the
Jew hopes.
I am a Jew because the promise of Israel is the universal
promise.
I am a Jew because, for Israel, the world is not yet
completed: men are completing it.
I am a Jew because, above the nations and Israel, Israel
places Man and his Unity.
I am a Jew because, above Man's image of the divine Unity,
Israel places the divine Unity, and its divinity.

EDMOND FLEG

September 1982. Rosh Hashanah afternoon. I sit outdoors
with my son during a break in services. A year ago, at age
eleven, he decided that he wanted a bar mitzvah, after re-
jecting Hebrew school . . . years before. . . . We are listening

to the fountain play. My son asks what you have to do to be a *real* Jew. I remind him that we have just finished reading a handout from an essay of Martin Buber's which explains that there is no single correct way to be a Jew, but that each individual has his or her own right path to God. He asks, reasonably, how you find out what the right path is for you. You listen, I tell him, to your inner voice, through which God speaks to you. He looks puzzled, as well he might. I am on the spot. Then I get it. Your inner voice, I tell him, is what made you want the bar mitzvah, and what made you *nudge* Dad and me until we took you seriously. He looks blank a moment longer, and then he nods, yes. And yes, in the absence of any more plausible explanation, I, too, suppose God instructed Gabe.

ALICIA OSTRIKER

Mine is the Judaism of the deed. It's the Judaism of Abraham Isaac Kook, the Ashkenazi Chief Rabbi of pre-State Palestine, who sees holiness as an intensified form of life itself. It's the Judaism of the philosopher Martin Buber, who called for "the life of dialogue" and debate, not monologue and dogma. It's the Judaism of Abraham Joshua Heschel, the pre-eminent American rabbi, who came home from Selma, Alabama, and said, "When I marched with Martin Luther King, I felt as if my legs were praying." It's the Judaism of Rabbi Marshall Meyer, who in the 1970s put his life on the line to protect victims of state terrorism in Argentina. And it is the Judaism of thousands of ordinary and extraordinary women—activists, rabbis, scholars, writers, ritualists, community organizers— who define female Jews as *full* Jews, and who work to expand women's role in Jewish life.

What I'm describing here is . . . a rigorous and demanding [Judaism] that asks us to "act Jewish" in the world. It demands that we repair the world, little by little, day after day, by actively pursuing justice and peace, and battling against cruelty and inequity. Also that we speak out about the human condition with the aim of improving it.

LETTY COTTIN POGREBIN

I consider a maximum Jew a person who really lives with Jewishness. It is his whole life. When I think about a maximum Jew, I think about my father because I knew him best. For this man, being a Jew and being a human being were the same thing. When my father wanted to say that a person has to eat, he would say "a Jew has to eat"—not because he thought that the Gentiles should not eat, but because a Jew and a person were for him synonymous. To our parents and grandparents, this was their life. Jewishness was actually the very air they breathed.

. . . There are many grades of Jewishness, and I think that this is the way also that our sages have understood it, because they said, *"Yisrael aff al piy she'chata Yisrael hu"*—a Jew, even if he has sinned, is still a Jew. And even a man who has converted to Christianity is considered a Jew from the point of view of religion. This is the meaning of maximum and minimum Jews.

ISAAC BASHEVIS SINGER

Men may change their clothes, their politics, their wives, their religions, their philosophies, to a greater or lesser extent: they cannot change their grandfathers. Jews or Poles or Anglo-Saxons, in order to cease being Jews or Poles or Anglo-Saxons, would have to cease to be.

HORACE KALLEN

Within my heart, within my identity, there live many different Jews. There is the son of a Yiddish poet, the child of the

Yiddish tongue. There is the German Jewish boy who studied in Munich's Orthodox day school. There is the refugee from Nazi terrorism, who joined the Allied Jewish soldiers who helped demolish the Third Reich. There is the child of the Old World who was pulled along by his father to catch a glimpse of Chaim Weizman.

The multi-colored coat that is my Jewish identity is not an emblem of pride or personal attainment. It is simply a product of the threads of my life experience, indeed, of the threads of recent Jewish history.

ALEXANDER M. SCHINDLER

WHAT JUDAISM TEACHES

It takes three things to attain a sense of significant being:
God
A Soul
And a moment.
And the three are always here.
Just to be is a blessing. Just to live is holy.

ABRAHAM J. HESCHEL

Judaism teaches that this life, this earth, is God given and therefore good: that we are capable of achieving great and beautiful things through our own efforts, added to our divine endowment of our personalities. Judaism teaches that nobody stands between man and his creator, that the gates of heaven are open to us whenever we wish to approach them. The basis of Judaism is both faith and practice. Anyone who sincerely endeavors to live in accord with Jewish law may rightly be called a Torah-true Jew.

LEO JUNG

WE ARE A CONTINUANCE OF OUR PEOPLE

I was thought to be a Jew because I was so named by others. I learned by being one that "Jew" is more than epithet. The content of tenuous community, risk, and history makes me feel immortal even though I'm not. No matter what happens to me, I am continuous with a past which was worthy of better than me; a present when others died to be Jews; a future constructed equally of fate and intention. . . . I am a part of history, not merely a kid on a street corner or a man making out okay.

HERBERT GOLD

Every Jew must act as if he or she personally had gone forth from Egypt.

THE *MISHNAH*

This Jewish community has a remarkable past. It walks around with two thousand years of history on its back. . . . It is separated from the outside world as though it were an island in the middle of an ocean, and what goes on in that world is like a splashing of surf that never reaches higher than the ankles. The members of this community are bound and shackled to one another, and should one of them wish to break away, he has no choice but to cast himself into the waves, which will carry him apart from the Jewish world forever.

BAᶜAL MAKHSHOVES

I am asked why I am a Jew. It is to you, my grandson, who are not yet born, that I would make my reply.

. . . When will you be born? In ten years, perhaps fifteen.

. . . What form will the world then take? Will the mechanical have suppressed the spiritual? Will the mind have created a new universe for itself? Will the problems that trouble me to-day exist for you? Will there be any Jews left?

I believe there will. They have survived the Pharaohs, Nebuchadnezzar, Constantine, Mohammed; they have survived the inquisition and assimilation; they will survive the automobile.

But you, my child, will you be a Jew? People say to me: You are a Jew because you were born a Jew. You did not will to be one; you cannot change that. Will this explanation suffice for you, if, born a Jew, you no longer feel that you are a Jew?

I myself, at the age of twenty, thought I had no further interest in Israel. I was convinced that Israel would disappear, that in twenty years people would no longer speak of it. Twenty years have passed, and twelve more, and I have again become a Jew.

That which happened to me may happen to you also, my child. If you believe that the flame of Israel is extinguished within you, pay heed and wait; some day it will be rekindled. It is a very old story, which begins anew each century. Israel has had a thousand opportunities to die; a thousand times it has been reborn. I want to tell to you how it died and was reborn in me, so that, if it dies in you, you in turn may experience its rebirth.

Thus I will have brought Israel to you, and you will bring it to others if you will, if you can. And we two in our way will have treasured and transmitted the divine behest: "These words which I command thee shall be upon thy heart and upon thy soul; bind them as a sign upon thy hand and let them be as frontlets between thine eyes. You shall teach them to your children. . . ."

EDMOND FLEG

Chicago, 1958. We heard this on the news: *Mike Todd, producer, impresario, husband of Elizabeth Taylor, is dead in a plane crash.*

My mother and aunt sit at the dining room table, discussing his death in hushed and sorrowful tones. *My bubbe* probably sewing, although I have no concrete memory of her movements, pays no attention until one of them mentions that he is to be buried at Waldheim Cemetery. "Waldheim?" she asks. "He was Jewish?" Suddenly Mike Todd matters to her, belongs to her family. She mourns him like a long-lost son.

BONNIE ZIMMERMAN

RESPONSIBILITY FOR ALL

All Jews are responsible one for another.

BABYLONIAN TALMUD, SHEVUOT 39A

Some people were sitting in a ship, when one of them took a drill and began to bore a hole under his seat. The other passengers protested to him, "What are you doing?" He answered, "What has this to do with you? Am I not boring the hole under my own seat?"

They retorted, "But the water will come in and drown us all."

LEVITICUS RABBAH 4:6

It is a grave responsibility this—to be a Jew; and you can't escape from it, even if you choose to ignore it. Ethically or religiously, we Jews can be and do nothing light-heartedly. Ten bad Jews may help to damn us; ten good Jews may help to save us. Which minyan will you join?

CLAUDE G. MONTEFIORE

MITZVAH

A *mitzvah* is like a musical score. Its performance is not a mechanical accomplishment but an artistic act. The music in a score is open only to him who has music in his soul. It is not enough to play the notes; one must be what he plays. It is not enough to do the mitzvah; one must live what he does.

ABRAHAM J. HESCHEL

Our religion does not deal with never-never lands, platforms of impossible ideals. It offers neither a cosmic fancy nor any connection with devils, demons and ghosts. One is not a good Jew by conforming to the ritual alone, or by giving charity alone, or by observing high standards in social relations. The goal of a good Jew must be total performance of the *mitzvah*.

LEO JUNG

THE JEWISH HOME

The Jewish home has been called a *mikdash ma'at*, a little sanctuary. It is an evocative image. From the moment you walk through the doorway of a sanctuary, you know you are entering a place that cries the idea that space is always neutral.

No sanctuary is perpetually filled with all the beauty or meaning it might contain. No home is ever fully or finally a sanctuary. But the ongoing process of making Jewish choices is what makes a home into a *mikdash ma'at*, an island of peace, a safe harbor, a beautiful Jewish place.

ANITA DIAMANT

The Jew's home has rarely been his "castle." Throughout the ages it has been something far greater—his sanctuary.

JOSEPH H. HERTZ

Ours was a distinctly Jewish household, even though we never attended a synagogue, even though my sister and I were never taught the rudiments of the Jewish religion. On Jewish festivals my parents closed the store, not only in deference to what the neighbors might say but also out of a sense of Jewish solidarity. My sister and I stayed home from school. My mother fasted on Yom Kippur, the Day of Atonement, on the grounds that it was healthy to fast once in a while, but she never appreciated the solemnity of that day. On Passover we got new clothes to wear, mostly sewn by my mother, our observance of the festival seemed like a Jewish version of the Easter Parade. I don't remember that we ever had a traditional *seder* at home, though we sometimes went to one in a relative's house. The one practice of Judaism my mother strictly followed was to buy kosher meat and poultry, which she never cooked in butter or milk. Sabbath observance was reduced to general house cleaning on Fridays. After she washed the kitchen floor, my mother spread the previous day's Yiddish newspapers over it to keep it from getting dirty right away.

LUCY DAWIDOWICZ

A Woman of Valor, Who Can Find? For Her Price Is Way Above Rubies

Israel is redeemed because of the pious women of the generation.

YALKUT SHIMONI

Be careful not to cause woman to weep, for God counts her tears.

TALMUD

In what lies the merit of women? In bringing their sons to study at the synagogue, in letting their husbands study at the *Beit Ha-Midrash*, and in waiting for them to return home.

BABYLONIAN TALMUD, BERAKHOT 17A

Remembering My Mother

My mother worked [in the kitchen] all day long. We ate in it almost all meals except the Passover seder. . . . The kitchen gave a special character to our lives; my mother's character. All my memories of that kitchen are dominated by the nearness of my mother sitting all day long at her sewing machine, by the clacking of the treadle against the linoleum floor, by the patient twist of her right shoulder as she automatically pushed at the wheel with one hand or lifted her foot to free the needle . . . The kitchen was her life. Year by year, as I began to take in her fantastic capacity for labor and her anxious zeal, I realized it was ourselves she kept stitching together.

ALFRED KAZIN

From memory's spring flows a vision tonight,
My mother is kindling and blessing the light;
The light of Queen Sabbath, the heavenly flame,
That one day in seven quells hunger and shame.
My mother is praying and screening her face,
Too bashful to gaze at the Sabbath light's grace.

She murmurs devoutly, "Almighty, be blessed,
For sending Thy angel of joy and of rest,
"And may as the candles of Sabbath divine
The eyes of my son in Thy law ever shine."
Of childhood, fair childhood, the years are long fled,
Youth's candles are quenched, and my mother is dead.
And yet every Friday, when twilight arrives,
The face of my mother within me revives;
A prayer on her lips, "O Almighty, be blessed,
for sending us Sabbath, the angel of rest."
And some hidden feeling I cannot control
A Sabbath light kindles deep, deep in my soul.

PHILIP RASKIN

WORLD OF OUR FATHERS

Let us now praise famous men. Our fathers in their generations.

ECCLESIASTES 44:1–15

Once I sat on the stairs at the gate of David's Tower, I placed my two heavy baskets at my side. A group of tourists was standing around their guide and I became their target marker.

(The guide spoke.) "You see that man with the baskets? Just right of his head, there's an arch from the Roman period. Just right of his head."

I said to myself: redemption will come only if their guide tells them: You see that arch from the Roman period? It's not important: but next to it, left and down a bit, there sits a man who bought fruit and vegetables for his family.

YEHUDA AMICHAI

THE DUTY TO HAVE CHILDREN

Then God blessed Adam and Eve and said: be fruitful and
multiply and fill the earth.

GENESIS 1

DEFINING A CHILD AS JEWISH

Why should a movement that from its birth-hour insisted on
the full equality of men and women in the religious life,
unquestioningly accept the principle that Jewish lineage is
valid through the maternal line alone? And all the more so
because there is substantial support in our tradition for the
validity of Jewish lineage through the paternal line!

Just as one example, both the Torah and rabbinic law hold
the male absolutely dominant in matters affecting the priest-
hood. Whether one is *cohen* or a *levi* depends on the father's
priestly claim, not the mother's. Well, if the father is good
enough to bequeath the priestly status, why isn't he good
enough to bequeath Jewishness?

ALEXANDER M. SCHINDLER

A PARENT'S LOVE

*David, an orphaned young man raised by a loving aunt and
uncle, goes off to enter the American army as a chaplain. On
the day he leaves, they escort him to the train station.*

David grabbed their rough peddler's hands in his smooth student ones. "How can I ever begin to repay you for what you've
done for me!"

Uncle Asher spoke gently: "There's a saying, 'The love of

parents goes to their children, but the love of these children goes to their children.' "

"That's not so!" David protested. "I'll always be trying to . . ."

Tante Dvorah interrupted, "David, what your Uncle Asher means is that a parent's love isn't to be paid back; it can only be passed on."

HERBERT TARR, *THE CONVERSION OF CHAPLAIN COHEN*

A Jewish man with parents alive is a fifteen-year-old boy and will remain a fifteen-year-old boy until they die.

PHILIP ROTH, *PORTNOY'S COMPLAINT*

If you do not let your son grow up as a Jew, you deprive him of those sources of energy which cannot be replaced by anything else. He will have to struggle as a Jew and you ought to develop in him all the energy he will need for the struggle. Do not deprive him of that advantage.

SIGMUND FREUD

TEACH YOUR CHILDREN

Teach your children in youth, and they will not teach you in your old age.

YIDDISH MAXIM

Soon a poorly clad couple entered, the man carrying in his arms a young boy of about six, wrapped in a *tallit*. Both father and mother were weeping with joy, grateful to God who had preserved them that they might witness this beautiful moment. Having extended a cordial welcome to the newcomers, the *melamed* took the hero of the celebration into his arms and stood him upon a table. Afterwards the boy was seated on a bench and was the first to receive cake, nuts, raisins and dainties of which the happy mother had brought along an apron-full. The teacher then sat down near the youngster, placed a card with a printed alphabet before him and, taking a long pointer, began the first lesson by blessing his newly-initiated pupil that he may be raised for the study of Torah, marriage, and good deeds.

LOUIS GREENBERG

You shall love the Lord, your God, with all your heart, with all your soul, and with all your might. And these words which I command you this day shall be upon your heart. And you shall teach them diligently to your children. . . .

DEUTERONOMY 6:4

Religious Education

Learning-learning-learning:
    That is the secret of Jewish survival.

AHAD HA'AM

There is no other way. The survival of a minority is a matter of nurture, not nature. It is sustained through education, nothing else. So long as Jews learned, they lived. Once they stopped learning, Jewish identity started dying.

JONATHAN SACKS

Whoever teaches his son teaches not alone his son but also his son's son, and sons to the end of generations.

BABYLONIAN TALMUD

GROUNDBREAKING DEDICATION: HEBREW UNIVERSITY, 1917

It seems at first paradoxical that in a land with so sparse a population, in a land where everything still remains to be done, in a land crying out for such simple things as ploughs, roads and harbors, we should begin by creating a center of spiritual and intellectual development. But it is no paradox for those who know the soul of the Jew.

CHAIM WEIZMANN

THE HEBREW LANGUAGE

To the religious Jew, Hebrew is the language of worship. . . . To men of letters, Hebrew is the key to a classic literature which records the intimate experiences and memories of an ancient people. To lovers of Israel, Hebrew can serve as a bond of unity with world Jewry and the state of Israel. To Jewry at large, Hebrew can serve as a potent factor in Jewish survival, for it links the Jew to his past, binds him to the present, and enables him to share in the vision for a creative Jewish life in the future.

SAMUEL M. BLUMENFELD

Flowing down from the hills of eternity, the Hebrew language has been set apart by God as the receptacle of truths destined to sway mankind and humanize the world.

SABATO MORAIS

THE PEOPLE OF THE BOOK

The early Hebrews had created the Bible out of their lives;
their descendants created their lives out of the Bible.

ABRAM LEON SACHAR

Is it a book, a world, a heaven?
Are those words, or flames, or shining stars,
Or burning torches, or clouds of fire
What is it, I ask ye—the Bible?

Who inspired those infinite truths?
Who spoke through the mouth of the prophet?
Who mapped out the highways of ages,
The glorious lines of the Scriptures?

Who planted the flowers of wisdom
In this sacred soil of the angels?
O dream of eternity—Bible
O Light that is all and forever.

MORRIS ROSENFELD

The Bible, what a book! Large and wide as the world, based
on the abysses of creation, and peering aloft into the blue
secrets of heaven; sunrise and sunset, promise and fulfillment,
birth and death, the whole drama of humanity are contained
in this one book.

. . . Nations rose and vanished, states flourished and de-
cayed, revolutions raged throughout the earth—but they, the
Jews, sat poring over this book, unconscious of the wild chase
of time that rushed on above their heads.

HEINRICH HEINE

It has been said that a knowledge of the Bible without a college education is better than a college education without a knowledge of the Bible. One can learn more about human nature by reading the Bible than by living in the largest city.

PHILIP BIRNBAUM

Yiddish for the Ages

Yiddish, begins (so far as recent scholarship has reconstructed it) in the tenth and eleventh centuries, when Jews from Northern France came down the Rhineland, where they picked up the Germanic dialects of places in which they sank roots: Cologne, Trier, Coblenz, Mainz. Jews who filtered farther eastward learned the regional parlance of Frankfurt, Wurzburg, and Stuttgart. So grew up a vernacular, Judaeo-German, that was to become the foundation of Yiddish. And when Jews were invited (!) to come to reside in Poland, to form an economic class between ignorant peasants and indolent noblemen, they brought Hebrew and German with them. It was in the settlements of Middle and Eastern Europe—in Galacia, Hungary, Rumania, the Ukraine, Poland, Russia, Lithuania—that, after the seventeenth century, a unique Jewish language flowered and a novel literature grew up.

. . . the Jewish masses clung to their beloved vernacular, and embroidered and enriched it *ad libitum* . . . Hebrew, after all, was "God's tongue," far too sacred to be demeaned by earthly, earthy uses. More and more, Yiddish became the workaday tongue for everyday life, for sharing the vicissitudes of daily and domestic affairs.

LEO ROSTEN

I teach Yiddish still, at 86 years old. To all who will learn, I teach. And why? Because for us who left Europe with nothing—our language was our only possession. The only thing they could not take from us.

HASSIA SIEGEL

Mein Yiddishe meydele
Zie is azoy sheyn
Mein Yiddish meydele
Mit a Yiddish cheyn
My Jewish little girl is so beautiful,
My Jewish little girl with her Jewish charm.
(Song my Russian grandmother sang to me.—ed.)

FAITH: THE GRANDEST MYSTERY OF ALL

Faith is that attitude, part gift, part victory hard won, that allows each of us to look into our children's eyes, full of trust and purity, expectation and a little fear, and say to them, "I am so glad that I was able to bring you into this world." . . . Faith is what causes us to hum absent-mindedly, and to dream about tomorrow, though tomorrow may never come. Faith may just be the grandest mystery of all. And who in this world doesn't love a mystery?

NINA BETH CARDIN

Faith is real only when it is not one-sided but reciprocal. Man can rely on God, if God can rely on man. We may trust in Him because He trusts in us. Our trustworthiness for God is the measure of the integrity of our faith.

ABRAHAM J. HESCHEL

GOODNESS IS THE CENTRAL THEME

TIKKUN OLAM—REPAIRING THE WORLD

I had this idea that Jews were supposed to be better. I'm not saying they were, but they were supposed to be; and it seemed to me on my block that they often were. I don't see any reason in being in this world actually if you can't in some way be better, repair it somehow . . .

GRACE PALEY

Tikkun olam is our quest to bring the world of everyday life into a unity with the world on high, to build a Jacob's Ladder between human reality and human ideals. There are sparks of holiness imprisoned in the stuff of creation. Freeing these fragments and reuniting them with God—that is what *tikkun olam* is all about: gathering the sparks, searching for God in every corner of the world, restoring the divine unity. When we use our resources as blessings . . . when we treat other human beings as human beings . . . the sparks leap together. Then we know that our God is a living God; and in that knowledge we too come alive.

ALEXANDER M. SCHINDLER

The Jewish way in the world has consistently and unswervingly pursued the idea and technique of the good life. Not beauty but goodness is the central problem and theme of Judaism.

TRUDE WEISS-ROSMARIN

Free will is bestowed on every human being. If he desires to turn towards the good path and be just, he has the power to do so. If he wishes to turn towards the evil path and be wicked, he is at liberty to do so. And thus it is written in the Torah, "Behold, the man is become as one of us, to know good and evil" (Gen. 3:22) which means that the human species stands alone in the world—there being no other kind like him as regards this subject of being able of his own accord, by the reason and thought to know what is good and what is evil, with none to prevent him from either doing good or evil.

MOSES MAIMONIDES, *MISHNE TORAH*

For the Liberal Jew, it is not God who demands behavior of us so that we can know God, but rather we who demand behavior of ourselves so that we can discover the divine in life and in the world in which we live. We demand of ourselves that we be ethical and just, that we strive to touch another human life to make it better. We demand of ourselves that we work for peace and harmony, that we be committed not only to the people of Israel and to the ancient land from which we sprang, but that we commit ourselves to the good of all people because every human being contains a spark of the Divine.

ALAN D. FUCHS

TZEDAKAH — CHARITY

If there is one area that identifies and unites Jews, no matter what their personal beliefs and practices, it is *Tzedakah*. *Tzedakah* is more than charity or philanthropy, noble as they are; more than man's humanity to man, exalted as that is; more truly, it is righteousness and justice.

Without these qualities civilization would perish.

It is the highest ideal in Jewish teaching—for it is the highest application of Jewish ethical values. It is Judaism in action—and Judaism is inherently and deeply a religion of action, a way of life, a way of living.

PHILIP BERNSTEIN

Winter Sunday mornings in Detroit, my father and I would walk to the Warsaw Bakery on Twelfth Street to buy bagels. . . . No matter how early we came, the *Pushke* Lady was there before us, sitting in a chair safely out of the draft, shaking her canister under our noses. Jewish National Fund, Pioneer Women, Hadassah, Milk for Jewish Orphans, Trees for Palestine—thanks to the *Pushke* Lady, no Jew would have to slather cream cheese on his bagel with a guilty conscience.

Our house was a regular stop for pious men in need of a kosher meal who might find themselves without time enough to reach Detroit or Chicago before sundown of a Friday night. . . . What has become of them, those grizzled men in long black coats, poring over yellowed prayer books by the light of our living room window on *Shabbes* mornings so long ago? My mother would believe they were in heaven now, saying prayers for all of us.

The children grew, and I collected: Dollars for Democrats, March of Dimes on Roosevelt's birthday, UNICEF on Halloween. Later, the *Pushke* Lady syndrome became more complicated. When my oldest daughter was sixteen, I took her with me to the Alabama State capital to meet the Freedom Marchers who had walked from Selma to Montgomery. We both still remember the voice of Martin Luther King floating over our heads in the electric air and the long, sober train ride back with blinds drawn and lights out for fear of snipers. I didn't tell my daughter the trip was a *mitzvah* or even that it was part of her *pushke* training, but she knows it now.

FAYE MOSKOWITZ

There are eight degrees in the giving of charity, one higher than the other.

1. The highest degree, than which there is nothing higher, is to take hold of a person who has been crushed and to give

him a gift or a loan, or to enter into partnership with him, or to find work for him, and thus put him on his feet that he will not be dependent on his fellow men.

2. Lower in degree to this is the one who gives charity, *tzedakah,* to the poor, but does not know to whom he gives it, nor does the poor man know from whom he received it . . .

3. Lower in degree to this is when the giver knows to whom he gives, but the poor does not know from whom he receives . . .

4. Lower in degree to this is when the poor knows from whom he receives, but the giver does not know to whom he gives . . .

5. Lower in degree to this is when one gives even before he is asked . . .

6. Lower in degree to this is when one gives after he has been asked . . .

7. Lower in degree to this is when one gives less than he should, but graciously . . .

8. Lower in degree to this is when one gives grudgingly . . .

MOSES MAIMONIDES, *MISHNE TORAH*

WITH JUSTICE FOR ALL

. . . The demand for justice runs through the entirety of the Jewish tradition.

RUTH BADER GINSBURG

Judaism has had a very profound effect on me. Jews believe you can't have justice for yourself unless other people have justice as well. That has motivated much of what I've done.

BELLA ABZUG

TRUTH

The Hasidic Rebbe, Elimelekh of Lyzhansk said:
When I die and stand in the court of justice, they will
ask me if I had been as just as I should have been.
I will answer no.

Then they will ask me if I had been as charitable as I should
have been.
I will answer no.

Did I study as much as I should have?
Again, I will answer no.

Did I pray as much as I should have?
And this time, too, I will have to give the same answer.

Then the Supreme Judge will smile and say:
"Elimelekh, you spoke the truth. For this alone you have a share
in the world to come."

TALE ABOUT ELIMELECH OF LYZHANSK (1717–1787)

ANTI-SEMITISM

A few years ago, a justice of the Supreme Court of the United
States declared that while he could not define obscenity, he
knew it when he saw it. That is the way we Jews feel about anti-
Semitism. We definitely know it when we read it, see it or hear
it, and we certainly feel it when it breeds violence against us.

ABRAHAM FOXMAN

No matter whether or not you believe in God, read Hebrew,
fast on Yom Kippur, or support Israel, the anti-Semites know
you are Jewish. They will come for you anyway.

BONNIE ZIMMERMAN

Prejudice works harm in both directions, to the objects of it, and to those who entertain it. The objects of prejudice, when sensitive, are led to shrink back within racial lines. . . . But those who entertain the prejudice are no less harmed. It has been truly said that no one can shut out other folks without shutting himself in, and shutting himself in often within very narrow and narrowing bounds. . . . And how should the prejudice be met? When Plato was told that men spoke evil of him, he answered, I must then so live that they will be compelled to change their tune.

FELIX ADLER

Before we can effectively combat anti-Semitism, we must first of all educate ourselves out of it, and out of the slave-mentality which it betokens. Only when we respect ourselves, can we win the respect of others; or rather, the respect of others will then come of itself.

ALBERT EINSTEIN

I'VE KEPT MY NAME

I find that keeping my name, far from complicating my life, simplifies it. I was born an American and a Jew. . . . I am what I am as you are what you are. . . . It wouldn't be wholly admirable if I should, by changing my name, reject the fifty centuries' history and tradition of my people in order to gain a hotel room at Newport.

DAVID L. COHN

ONE GOD

In the belief in God, the history of Judaism gains its meaning, its heroic significance. Only he who sees the source and destination of his existence in the one and only God has experienced Judaism. He also is truly a Jew who, in the face of eternity, when the soul hears itself called to its God and when it is embraced by the infinite, is able to pronounce as the outcome and confession of his life The Words which the genius of Israel has shaped for the hours of decision and departure: "Hear, O Israel, the Lord our God, the Lord is One."

LEO BAECK

God is not alone when discarded by men. But man is alone.

ABRAHAM J. HESCHEL

We shall not come to experience the reality of God unless we go in search of Him. To be seekers of God, we have to depend more upon our own thinking and less upon tradition. Instead of acquiescing passively in the traditional belief that there is a God, and deducing from that belief conclusions which are to be applied to human experience and conduct, we must accustom ourselves to find God in the complexities of our experience and behavior.

MORDECAI M. KAPLAN

"Where does God exist?" the Rebbe asked several of his followers.

"Everywhere," the surprised disciples responded.

"No," the Rebbe answered. "God exists only where man lets him in."

BABYLONIAN TALMUD

Two Jews, Three Opinions

Perhaps the essence most characteristic of Judaism and one found in no other religion, culture, or civilization is its *argumentative nature*. We are a civilization of arguers. We argue with God, about God, with each other, about each other, and about everything that matters. Abraham and Moses argued with God. The Prophets argued with God, kings and priests. The *Berdichev* rabbi sued God. Elie Wiesel put God on trial. . . . The Talmud is a collection of arguments, in which even the losing side is given great status.

How could anyone expect so dialogic a people to have one *substantive* essence or even one *substantive* answer to fundamental questions?

ALAN DERSHOWITZ

To Transform the World

The ultimate goal (of Judaism) is to transform the world into the kind of world God had in mind when He created it.

HAROLD KUSHNER

TWO

It's a Tradition!

The past is a part of every Jew's experience, not just the holidays but all throughout the year, "It is done as it was done," and "It is said as it was said," Jewish secular law and Jewish religious practices are all based on referrals back to tractates and commentaries of other centuries. This makes Jews continually the witnesses of their own past and gives the odd flavor to their reasoning, as if history were happening in both the vertical and the horizontal time line, as if things moved forward and stayed still at the same time.

ANNE ROIPHE

Together with its Sabbath days Judaism has created the solemn seasons which twine themselves round the year like a holy bond. By pointing to the true meaning of existence, these holidays help to hold our life together so that it does not disintegrate into a mere succession of days. . . .

LEO BAECK

WHEN WE HAD NO TEMPLE, no accoutrements, and even no books, we always had tradition. From antiquity to the present, Jews have transmitted their heritage by observing and celebrating Jewish rituals and holidays. Sharing milestones with the community is a grand part of our tradition. Marriage is celebrated as a public ceremony. A male child is named at his *Brith Milah* in the presence of a quorum, and a female is named in the synagogue in the presence of the congregation. During the seven-day mourning period, friends and family join the mourner at his or her home to sit *shivah*, to pay their condolences, offer prayers and comfort to the mourner.

The celebration of Jewish holidays is both ritual and traditional. *Shabbat*, the Hebrew word for Sabbath or Saturday, is the only sacred day in Judaism that comes each week. During *Shabbat*, we do not work, concentrating instead on the wonders of God and life itself. The first holiday in the Jewish calendar year is Rosh Hashanah, considered to be the birthday of the world. This holy time speaks not only of all the creations of God's hand, but also of human responsibility to care for and protect those creations. Yom Kippur, eight days later, is a day of fasting, prayer, and asking God to forgive us for the sins we have committed. The sins enumerated in a prayer said only on this day, alert the Jew to the condition of the world, at home and abroad, and remind the Jew of the responsibility for *tikkun olam*.

The three pilgrimage festivals, celebrated in ancient times by excursions to the Temple of Jerusalem, are Passover (Pesach), Sukkoth, and Shavuot. Passover marks the beginning of the festival of spring, and the time of deliverance of the Israelites from Egyptian slavery. The celebration of the seder at which we tell the stories and use symbolic foods is one of the most beloved by my family and many others as well. Shavout marks the harvest of the first fruits, and the Revelation of the Decalogue at Sinai. Sukkoth, the festival of booths, falls five days after Yom Kippur.

The festival Simchat Torah concludes the fall season. Celebrated at the end of Sukkoth, Simchat Torah commemorates the completion of the reading of the book of Deuteronomy, the last book in the Torah, and the immediate beginning of Genesis, the first, without a pause. Hanukkah (the festival of lights) marks the victory of the Maccabees over the Assyrian Greeks, and the liberation and rededication of the Temple in Jerusalem to the worship of God. To mark this great national event and the miracle of the Temple's supply of pure ritual oil that should have burned one day but burned eight, we kindle eight candles on the Hanukkah menorah.

Purim celebrates the deliverance of the Persian Jewish community from the evil designs of Prime Minister Haman. The story is conveyed in a manner similar to a vintage Hollywood western. The cast includes Mordecai, the loyal Jew; Esther, the Jewish woman who becomes Queen; King Ahashueros, the simple-minded ruler; and Haman, the wicked enemy of the Jewish people. To celebrate that deliverance, Jews are commanded to imbibe until they cannot distinguish between "blessed be Mordecai and cursed be Haman." The scroll of Esther is read in the synagogue, and everyone twirls their "grogger" to blot out the name and memory of Haman. We do not seek the death of Haman or the enemies of the Jewish people, only that their evil plans be changed. The telling and retelling of these historical accounts year after year conveyed to children and adults alike a connection to the past, a bond to the present, and a peek into the future.

Two other significant traditions (though not specific to life stages or the calendar) are noted in this chapter: Jewish humor and the changing role of women in Judaism. While humor has been a constant staple of Jewish liturgy since the days of the shtetl or earlier even, the role of women, at least modern women, continues to evolve.

In the earliest days, Jewish women were often considered second-class citizens. There is even a famous prayer in which a man thanks God daily "for not making me a woman." Women's inferior status had much to do with the ritual ancient Jewish law, which considered women, at certain times, to be ritually impure, a belief which cast them in a different position, a *secondary* position.

An additional rational behind the status of women in Judaism has to do with the *mitzvoth* regarding time and place. Because women are generally the ones to care for the children and the household, and because these obligations cannot be postponed or neglected, participation in fixed public prayer is unfeasible. On the other hand, these wifely and motherly tasks themselves may be considered as performance of an ongoing commandment, which would, by tradition, exempt women from performing other commandments, such as reciting prayers at specific times.

Jewish feminism first arose in the United States in the early 1970s as American women began to subject Judaism and the American Jewish community to feminist critiques. The Reform movement had, before that time, officially approved women's being included in the *minyan* and reading from the Torah, but it was not until the 1970s that these practices were acceptable in the synagogues. The Conservative movement allowed women to read from the Torah (*aliyah*) as far back as 1955, but they were not included in the *minyan* until the mid-seventies; however, decisions on these options were left up to the individual synagogues. This only made for confusion, as some synagogues became completely "integrated," while others allowed aliyah on some occasions (*bar* and *bas mitzvah*, for example) and not on others. The main reason the Orthodox community opposed equal access for women to the synagogue was that the public performance of prayer and To-rah study was traditionally a masculine role. In fact, in some cases, the Orthodox continue to move toward stringency, rather than toward a liberalization of these traditions.

But this does not mean the Orthodox confer inferior status to women. On the contrary. The separation of women and men in orthodox synagogues has a far loftier rational. Our sages have described the synagogue as a place to pray "as one man and with one heart." For this to occur there can be no intrusion of interfering factors, which includes the emotional atmosphere created whenever men and women are present together. This does not necessarily imply the thoughts are sinful. Even warm feelings of love for children and wives can become disruptive when a person is praying. So rather than shutting women out or, as some have said, "exiling women to the gallery," the orthodox custom of setting women apart from men in the synagogue is intended to help the worshiper direct his or her heart and his or her thoughts to God and God alone.

Today, because we are all so technologically connected, what is happening in the modern world has made itself felt in the Jewish world. Allowing women to help comprise a *min-yan* is now occurring in the majority of conservative syna-gogues. So is the fact that an unprecedented number of American women are being ordained as rabbis and cantors. Women are presidents of synagogues and sit on synagogue boards. Even in the Modern Orthodox Jewish world, women who are devoutly religious are fighting for, and gaining, new autonomy within the tradition.

Humor was, and still is, connected to the Jewish experi-ence in large part because it works so well as a defense mech-anism. People have always employed humor as a way of protecting themselves and to laugh in the face of adversity. A wonderful example of this is found in the Broadway musical *Fiddler on the Roof* where Tevya cries out in public: "May God bless and keep the Czar—far away from us!" That kind of humor did not necessarily belittle the enemy, but rather set up a scenario in which Jews laughed at themselves and took their minds off all their problems. They felt the pathos of life and found humor in the sadness. Although centuries now separate us from the days of the *shtetl*, Jewish humor endures. Which makes one wonder: Was the *shtetl* a harbinger of the Catskills? Think: Brice, Berle, Youngman, Klein, Saul, Fields, Benny, Burns, Storch, Brooks, Reiner, Allen, Radner, Mason, Rivers, and Seinfeld. Why are comedians so often Jewish? Why are Jews so often comedians? Don't ask!

*   *   *

THE LIFE CYCLE

THOUGHTS AT THE BIRTH OF A NEW-BORN INFANT

Just born and he already enjoys the longest genealogical record in the Western World. Was he not admitted to the "Covenant of Abraham"? So-called blue bloods and their social register are upstarts and parvenus alongside of this little fellow. And the list of his ancestors is studded with the prominent names of creative spirits who enriched the life of all mankind. He seems a little frail to bear so great a patrimony. Yet what possibilities he represents.

He has a capacity for such attachment to Jewish traditions as to enhance his life and to acquire a sense of deep companionship with Jews everywhere.

He can be a good American imbued with profound democratic sensitivities and with a fine awareness of the interdependence of all men.

He is qualified to join in a beautiful synthesis of the two currents of influence in his life, the Judaic and the American.

The symbols of Judaism can add beauty to his daily life and its culture can enrich his ethical and intellectual background.

He can enter American life proudly and with dignity unbent by the centuries of Jewish deprivation, and unhurt by underground streams of misconception and bigotry.

He can feel kinship with the great Jewish communities of the past, without ignoring the fact that the American Jewish settlement must respect the logic of its particular climate and background.

He can hold strongly to convictions without defaming those who differ.

He can live by a system of high values without surrendering in the name of modernity, to the vulgarities and errors from which no society is totally free.

He can be versed in the Bible and help reinstate the Jew as a "People of the Book."

He can build a home, that is not simply a stereotyped copy of the homes of his class, but possesses the distinctive qualities of his Jewishness and the best features of American life.

He can be a faithful Jew without being parochial and a loyal American without being the less Jewish.

What an opportunity he represents!

MORRIS ADLER

Pledge to Our Adopted Child: A Prayer

We have been blessed with the precious gift of a child. After so much waiting and wishing, we are filled with wonder and with gratitude as we call you our daughter/son. Our son/daughter, our child, you have grown to life apart from us, but now we hold you close to our hearts and cradle you in our arms with our love. We welcome you into the circle of our family and embrace you with the beauty of a rich tradition.

We pledge ourselves to the creation of a Jewish home and to a life of compassion for others, hoping that you will grow to cherish and emulate these ideals.

God of new beginnings, teach us to be mother and father, worthy of this sacred trust of life. May our daughter/son grow in health, strong in mind and kind in heart, a lover of Torah, a seeker of peace. Bless all of us together within your shelter of *Shalom*.

SANDY EISENBERG SASSO

BRITH: A SWIFT AND DELICATE ART

Eight days after he is born, a Jewish boy makes acquaintance with one of Judaism's most venerable institutions: *the mohel.* Technically, any competent Jew can be a *mohel*, the one who circumcises infant boys, but a good *mohel* is usually a specialist who has mastered a swift and delicate art.

The circumcision ceremony is called *bris*, meaning covenant. In Genesis 17:11, God promises to bless Abraham and all of his children if he, in turn, will be loyal to God. Their covenant is sealed with a sign that cannot be hidden: "Circumcise the flesh of your foreskin, and that shall be the mark of the Covenant between you and Me." Four thousand years later, the *bris* remains one of the oldest consistently observed rituals known to humanity.

DAVID COHEN

BRINGING A BABY GIRL INTO THE COVENANT

It is a *mitzvah* to give a child a Hebrew name. This name should be announced and the child blessed in the synagogue. The naming ceremony usually takes place at a regular Sabbath or daily service at the earliest time after the birth of the child when both parents can attend, (generally) within two months of birth.

GATES OF MITZVAH

As I write this, the birth of my first child is two months away. Thanks to modern science we know the sex—a girl. We have also been given a due date: November 10. It is the date of our wedding anniversary; it is also the anniversary of *Kristallnacht*, the event that shattered my father's world and helped usher in the unspeakable tragedy of the twentieth century.

My sister was given the name of my father's murdered

mother, just as I was named for his murdered father. In Ashkenazic Jewish tradition, a name possessed by the living cannot be given away. And so it is the name of my mother's mother that I will pass on to my child.

JONATHAN ROSEN

May You, who blessed our mothers
Sarah, Rebekah, Rachel and Leah,
bless her who has given birth,
together with her daughter, born in a happy
hour. Let her name be called in Israel
_____ bat _____
May her parents have the merit of leading
her to the Torah, to the wedding canopy,
and to good deeds. And let us say amen.

PRAYER FOR A BABY GIRL AT HER "NAMING" CEREMONY

BLESSING FOR ALL CHILDREN

May you live to see your world fulfilled
May your destiny be for worlds still to come,
And may you trust in generations past and yet to be.
May your heart be filled with intuition
And your words be filled with insight.
May songs of praise ever be upon your tongue
And your vision be a straight path before you.
May your eyes shine with the light of holy words
And your face reflect the brightness of the
heavens . . .

TALMUD, BERACHOT 17A

God commands us to perform countless acts of love.

How can we begin to obey such a difficult commandment? It is not such a mystery really.

Every lullaby, every diaper change, every smile, every sleepless night, every wordless prayer of thanks for this perfect baby—in these and the unending ways we care for and teach and protect our children, we perform countless acts of love.

And the world is made holier. And so are we.

THE MIDRASH

Bat Mitzvah Prayer

I write these words just a month before my own daughter becomes a bat mitzvah. I hope to tell her:

"There was a time when women were told what they could *not* be. Then there came a time when women were told what they *needed* to be, if they wanted success. But I want you to know: There is nothing as a woman you cannot be, and there are two things you need to be—true to yourself and responsible to your community."

What I Wish For My Daughter, I Wish For All Our Children.

I wish for you to be a person of character
strong but not tough,
gentle but not weak.

I wish for you to be righteous but not self-righteous
honest but not unforgiving.
Wherever you journey, may your steps be firm
and may you walk in just paths
and not be afraid.

Whenever you speak, may your words
be words of wisdom and friendship.

May your hands build
and your heart preserve what is good
and beautiful in our world.

May the voices of the generations of our people
move through you
and may the God of our ancestors
be your God as well.

May you know that here is a people,
a rich heritage, to which you belong
and from that sacred place
you are connected to all who dwell on the earth.

May the stories of our people
be upon your heart
and the grace of the Torah rhythm
dance in your soul.

SANDY EISENBERG SASSO

THERE IS NO SUCH THING AS A BAR OR BAT MITZVAH CEREMONY WITHOUT TEARS

The tears belong to several people. They belong to parents who are swelling with pride and relief. They belong to grandparents who may come up for their *Aliyah*. They listen to their grandchild read or chant from the Torah, and by the time they utter the closing blessing, their lips are quivering and their tears are falling. I have seen tears fall right onto the Torah scroll. Of all the places where tears might fall, that is the holiest place of all.

JEFFREY SALKIN

WEDDINGS

"SUNRISE, SUNSET"

Is this the little girl I carried,
Is this the little boy at play
I don't remember getting older,
When did they?

When did she get to be a beauty?
When did he grow to be so tall?
Wasn't it yesterday when they were
small?

Sunrise, sunset,
Sunrise, sunset.
Quickly fly the years.
One season following another
Laden with happiness and tears.

JEROME BOCK AND SHELDON HARNEK,
FIDDLER ON THE ROOF

Visitor at a Hasidic Wedding: Brooklyn, 1996

The actual marriage ceremony takes place on the sidewalk in front of the wedding hall, in keeping with the custom of being married under the stars. Hasidim crowd around as the bride circles the groom seven times. Meanwhile, the elevated train roars overhead, and a Hispanic couple argues on the opposite street corner.

Inside, the band has begun to play, accompanying a famous Hasidic singer, David Werdyger. The pint-sized Werdyger belts it out like Ethel Merman. He is wearing a *spodik*, a fur hat shaped like a bishop's miter that makes him look like an escapee from a

Moose Lodge initiation. The hat stands out in a sea of *shtreimels*, the less flamboyant hats made out of pelts of sable.

The men shuffle round and round in a circle. Several vigorously invite me to join. Soon we are circumambulating the groom, who charges back and forth against the inner edge of the circle arm-in-arm with his ninety-year-old grandfather. "Ninety years old and ninety grandchildren," somebody says.

The groom is hoisted up on a chair and the bride is brought out from behind the panels separating the women and the men. She too is hoisted up on a chair. The chairs are brought together, then apart, together, apart. Everyone is encouraged to dance. I am treated no differently than anyone else.

ROBERT EISENBERG

From every human being there rises a light that reaches straight to heaven. And when two souls that are destined to be together find each other, their streams of light flow together and a single brighter light goes forth from their united being.

BAʿAL SHEM TOV

Stacey and Stan's Kabbalastic Wedding Service, Livingston, New Jersey, April 1999.

It is written in the Kabbalah: As the earth encircles the sun and receives energy and warmth from it, so may your lives encircle each other, sharing warmth and energy one for the other. The Kabbalists taught, "Each soul and spirit, prior to its entering into this world, consists of a male and female united into one being. When it descends upon this earth, the two parts separate and animate two different bodies. Each individual thus becomes a "half-soul" which yearns to find its compliment in life.

In man and woman, God has planted the desire and the passion, to be joined to each other; ever pursuing and being pursued. For such is the blessing of love; without end and without limit. If the two individuals are pure and their conduct is pleasing in the sight of God, they are reunited under the wedding canopy.

Amen.

BARRY FRIEDMAN

Converting: Choosing Judaism

The Jewish attitude toward conversion has changed dramatically. Although tradition required that rabbis try to rebuff people interested in converting, today the door is wide open. Where conversion for the purpose of marriage was once treated as suspect, today rabbis and Jewish organizations welcome and even solicit interest from non-Jews planning to marry or already married to Jewish spouses.

In large part, this change is a response to the fact that as many as half of all American Jews marry non-Jews, and thus the fear that there will be no "next generation" of American Jews. There is also a renewed and self-confident sense that Judaism is an intrinsically fulfilling way of life that appeals to people for many different reasons. For whatever reason it is pursued, however, choosing Judaism is a major and momentous decision. One who makes this decision seriously and sincerely is called a "righteous proselyte" or *ger tzedek*, from the same root as *tzadik*, or "righteous/holy person."

ANITA DIAMANT

The *MIKVEH*

You can bring nothing to the *mikveh*, only yourself.

You come utterly naked, a physical manifestation of a spiritual reality.

Naked of all your accomplishments.

Naked of all your relationships to others.

Naked of all your defense mechanisms.

You cannot even bring your name. . . .

If you are truly honest, you will admit that when stripped

of all these things, there is not really very much of "you" left. You cannot see why that self should be acceptable to God or the Jewish people.

So, naked and exposed, you are in the most profound sense accepting. You cannot be anything else.

And you are, in the same moment, accepted.

You arise from the water, clothed with the *mitzvot* as a garment of light.

Having gone through it, you will never, ever be the same.

PAULA REIMERS

It is a mitzvah to admit into the Jewish community any person who wishes sincerely to adopt Judaism and who is willing to study it and accept its *mitzvot.*

The Jewish people have accepted *geirim* since biblical times. Ruth, the great-grandmother of King David, was a Moabite, and it was she who first enunciated the standard for entry into Judaism: "Your people shall be my people, and your God my God" (Ruth 1:16).

GATES OF MITZVAH

When a Marriage Ends

When a marriage ends, the altar sheds tears.

BABYLONIAN TALMUD

Friday night . . . was a time when, by the magic of the Sabbath candles, we were transformed into a happy, picture-book family. The recriminations and bickering would cease and the music would begin . . . Shalom (my brother), and I would sit at the gleaming white table in our "Shabbat outfits," dark blue pants and white cotton shirts open at the collar. Our hair was still wet from our pre-Sabbath baths, and it was combed neatly across our foreheads. Yarmulkes were bobby-pinned to our heads. My mother waved her hands over the lighted candles and covered her eyes as she stood in a silent moment of meditation. Afterwards, she took us into her arms and kissed us, lingering an extra moment to drink in our freshness. She told us that we looked like the two angels that tradition says accompany the men home from the Friday-night service.

When, a little while later, my father returned from the synagogue, we lined up in front of him for the Sabbath blessing, the eldest, Shalom, first and then me. "May God make you like Ephraim and Menashe," he said, invoking the two grandsons of Jacob who, as Joseph's children, were especially beloved. Bending down to reach us, my father cradled our heads between his strong hands as he recited the blessing. "May He bless you and keep you . . . and give you peace."

. . . On one such Friday night, I sensed the perfect opportunity. "I want a dog," I announced between songs.

"Not again," my mother said. "Sweetheart, I already told you, no dogs. Anyway, I think you're allergic to dogs."

"Judy," my father interrupted, "You don't know that for sure and besides, I don't see the harm . . ."

"Marvin." Her voice was rising. "Don't contradict me in front of the children." And that was the end of the singing. The music stopped and the candles went out.

Not long after, my parents were divorced. The fight over the dog, of course, had nothing to do with it. It was just another in a series and, no doubt, one of the more benign of their tortured nine-year marriage. But try telling that to a five-year-old boy.

All sons and daughters of divorce blame themselves. In their minds, the only way to expiate the guilt is to re-create what was lost. That is why each of us harbors a dream, the dream of bringing our parents back together again. On a subconscious level, this becomes our life's work. For me, the mission was to re-create a serenity and harmony of the Sabbath table. That was all I needed to do to restore our fall from Paradise.

ARI GOLDMAN

LOSS AND REMEMBRANCE

Later in the day, at the bottom of a bureau drawer in my father's bedroom, my brother came upon a shallow box containing two neatly folded prayer shawls. The older *tallis* I took home with me, and we buried him in the other. When the mortician, at the house, asked us to pick out a suit for him, I said to my brother: "A suit? He's not going to the office! No, no suit—it's senseless. He should be buried in a shroud," I said, thinking that was how Jews were buried traditionally. But as I said it, I wondered if a shroud was any less senseless—he wasn't Orthodox and his sons weren't religious at all—and if it wasn't pretentiously literary and a little hysterically sanctimonious as well. I thought how bizarrely out of character an urban earthling like my insurance-man father, a sturdy man rooted all his life in everydayness, would look in a shroud even while I understood that that was the idea. But as nobody opposed me and I hadn't the audacity to say, "Bury him naked," we used the shroud of our ancestors to clothe his corpse.

PHILIP ROTH

When does death really occur? In a sense, it is not when the heart stops beating but when the person is no longer remembered by anyone. And so, for the mourner, life becomes a struggle of memory versus forgetting.

JACK REIMER

Gregory, our first born son, was killed in Lebanon on June 9, 1982, the third day of Operation Shalom HaGalil. [I learned of his death] the following Tuesday, June 15, at 10:00 in the morning. By 4:00 that afternoon, my son, Neil, and I were on a plane to new York to make a connection to Israel.

On Thursday, at three in the afternoon, the traditional burial time in Israel, we walked slowly to the kibbutz coffee-house. Greg's body arrived from wherever it had been housed and lay in state in a flag-draped pine casket as all the adults in the kibbutz gathered outside. . . . We buried him in a traditional military ceremony. The *kibbutzniks* shoveled the earth into the grave; my brother helped. Eight women soldiers, not yet in their twenties, laid flowers on the grave. Rifles were fired tree times in his honor. Afterward, we all felt lighter, relieved. We left Israel the next morning.

Rabbi Friedman visited. We sat on the deck in the sunshine, and he said, "You know, now you are the *kaddish*. Usually the child is *kaddish* for the parents, but you are his *kaddish*." I did not know what he meant: the *Kaddish* is a prayer, not a person. Having been brought up as a reform Jew in a family that was highly assimilated, I had never heard the term *kaddish* used as the rabbi was now using it. "What do you mean?" I asked. He told me that it is the responsibility of the *kaddish* to keep the memory of the dead person alive, to not forget, not to let others forget.

PATRICIA Z. BARRY

The most famous story concerning Beruriah is that relating to the death of her two sons. They died suddenly on the Sabbath, and Beruriah withheld the news from her husband so as not to disturb his Sabbath peace. After *Havdalah*, the ceremony marking the end of Sabbath, Beruriah said to Rabbi Meir:

"Some time ago I was entrusted by a friend with some jewels for safekeeping and now he wants them back. Shall I return them?"

"Of course," answered Rabbi Meir, "the jewels must be returned."

Beruriah then took him to where their dead sons were lying. When he collapsed and cried, she gently reminded him: "Did you not say we must return to the owner the precious jewels he entrusted to us? The Lord has given the Lord has taken away. Blessed be the name of the Lord."

MIDRASH

On my father's Memorial Day
I went out to see his mates—
All those buried with him in one row,
His life's graduation class.

I already remember most of their names,
Like a parent collecting his little son
From school, all of his friends.

My father still loves me, and I
Love him always, so I don't weep.
But in order to do justice to this place
I have lit a weeping in my eyes
With the help of a nearby grave—
A child's. "Our little Yossi, who was
Four when he died."

YEHUDA AMICHAI

THE JEWISH CALENDAR

The Jewish Calendar is a lunar one, adapted to the solar year by various expedients . . . founded upon the calculations of the Greek astronomers. The month between one new moon and the next is reckoned as 29 days, 12 hours, 876 minutes . . . The years are grouped in cycles of 19, according to the system of Meton, a Greek astronomer of the fifth century B.C.

According to Jewish tradition, the present calendar was fixed by a Rabbi Hillel of Palestine, in A.D. 358, but there are certain indications that it went through further modifications after that date. In Biblical and early Talmudic times the new moons were fixed by actual observation, and were announced from Jerusalem to the surrounding countries.

THE JEWISH YEARBOOK — 5657 (1896)

THE SABBATH

"Remember the Sabbath Day to Keep It Holy." Six days shall you labor, and do all your work; but the seventh day is a Sabbath unto the Lord your God. In it you shall not do any manner of work, you, nor your son, nor your daughter, nor your man-servant, nor your maid-servant, nor your cattle, nor your stranger that is within your gates; for in six days the Lord made heaven and earth, the sea, and all that in them is, and rested on the seventh day; wherefore the Lord blessed the Sabbath day, and hallowed it.

EXODUS 20:8–11

As Israel has kept the Sabbath, so has the Sabbath kept Israel.

AHAD HA-AM

It was the darkness and emptiness of the streets I liked most about Friday evening, as if in preparation for that day of rest and worship which the Jews greet "as a bride"—that day when the very touch of money is prohibited, all work, all travel, all household duties, even to the turning on and off of a light—Jewry had found its way past its tormented heart to some ancient still center of itself. I waited for the streets to go dark on Friday evening as other children waited for the Christmas lights.

ALFRED KAZIN

It can be said that the six days of toil are concerned with the means of life and the Sabbath with the ends. The six days of toil represent the temporal and transitory—the Sabbath represents the eternal and the enduring. That is why the Hebrew language has no names for the days of the week—they are all the first day, or the second day, or the third day, "to the Sabbath"—the Sabbath is the goal toward which time itself moves. . . .

EMANUEL RACKMAN

THE NEW YEAR

This day [Rosh Hashanah] is a day of listening, perhaps with a new severity, a renewed attention. Can we listen to one another with the same attention that we accord to the shofar? Will we let the raucous shofar blasts startle us out of our complacency? Might we be able, maybe for the first time, to listen to our own voices and hear our own truths? For when we can hear our own breathing, our own heartbeats, the sound of our own blood pulsing through our veins, then we can begin to hear the essential humanity of those around us. Their cries, and moans, and laughter, will no longer be muted by the cacophony of our daily lives . . .

On this day of remembering, we shall remember. On this day of judgment, we will seek to become bringers of justice. On this day of listening, we will try very hard to listen to the still, small voice that inspires us toward acts of loving-kindness. And through such acts each of us can save the world.

SUE LEVI ELWELL

After my mother's death and despite my many spiritual detours, I never failed to attend *Shul* on Rosh Hashanah and Yom Kippur. The Jewish New Year was the real New Year; January first some pagan imitation.

So every autumn—even though these were my father's holidays, even when I felt angriest at him and at patriarchy, even when I lived alone in New York and answered to no one, even when I married my nonbeliever husband—I paid for a single ticket and went to stand with other Jews on the Days of Awe. Any synagogue would do, as long as it did not have a *mehitzah*.

All I needed was a Jewish space in which I could give strict account of my deeds, ask forgiveness from a God I felt owed me a favor, and say Kaddish for my mother. Every Rosh Hashanah, I put on my new fall clothes and took my place in some overflow service in some synagogue basement and ten days later, after Yom Kippur, this wandering worshiper disappeared from the Jewish community until the same time next year . . .

LETTY COTTIN POGREBIN

Although the sounding of the shofar on Rosh Hashanah is a decree of the Torah, it has a deep meaning as if saying: "Wake up from your deep sleep, you who are fast asleep . . . examine your souls, mend your ways and deeds."

MOSES MAIMONIDES

PRAYERS FOR THE HIGH HOLY DAYS

On Rosh Hashanah it is written and on Yom Kippur it is
*   sealed:*
How many shall leave this world and how many shall be born
*   into it*
who shall live and who shall die,
who shall live out the limits of his days and who shall not,
who shall perish by fire and who by water,
who by sword and who by beast,
who by hunger and who by thirst,
who by earthquake and who by plague,
who by strangling and who by stoning,
who shall rest and who shall wander,
who shall be at peace and who shall be tormented,

who shall be poor and who shall be rich
who shall be humbled and who shall be exalted.
But penitence, prayer and good deeds can annul the severity
of the decree.

MAZOR FOR THE HIGH HOLIDAYS

Remember us to life, O Soverign who delightest in life; inscribe us in the book of life for Your sake, O living God.

MAZOR FOR THE HIGH HOLIDAYS

AVINU MALKENU

Avinu Malkeynu, we have sinned before You.
Avinu Malkeynu, we have no Sovereign but You.
Avinu Malkeynu, abolish all evil decrees against us.
Avinu Malkeynu, rid us of every oppressor and adversary.
Avinu Malkeynu, bring us in perfect repentance to You.
Avinu Malkeynu, send a perfect healing to the sick among
Your people.
Avinu Malkeynu, inscribe us in the book for a good life.
Avinu Malkeynu, fill our hands with your blessings.
Avinu Malkeynu, have compassion on us and on our
children.
Avinu Malkeynu, grant us a good New Year.

MAZOR FOR THE HIGH HOLY DAYS

SUKKOT: THE AUTUMN FEAST

The holiday of *Sukkot* has two distinct origins. In pre-Biblical times, *Sukkot* was a harvest festival named after the temporary booths or huts built to shelter workers in the fields. Similar huts provided shelter for the Israelites during their forty-year flight from Egypt. Today, by re-creating the flimsy, hastily constructed *sukkot*, modern Jews both celebrate God's bounty

and commemorate His special concern for the Children of
Israel when He led them through a perilous wilderness.

DAVID COHEN

You shall live in booths seven days; all citizens in Israel shall
live in booths in order that future generations may know that
I made the Israelite people live in booths when I brought them
out of the land of Egypt, I the Lord your God.

LEVITICUS 23:42–43

We are back in the light of the full moon, the moon of the au-
tumnal equinox, the fifteenth of Tishri. Everything that the
earth will yield this year lies heaped in the storehouses: the
fruit, the grain, the wine, the oil: piles of yellow and green and
red, vats brimming purple and gold. The farmers of ancient Israel, like the farmers in all lands and times, gather for the
autumn Thanksgiving.

The full moon sheds its light on every man, woman and
child in Palestine. Nobody is indoors. The law of Moses requires that for seven days and nights all Jews live in huts
partially roofed by green boughs, palm branches, or piles of
reeds. In these frail structures the families feast, and sing,
and visit, and sleep. At the mercy of the weather, they live as
their ancestors did in the desert, in the first forty years of
independence, before they conquered Canaan.

HERMAN WOUK

The vineyards of Israel have ceased to exist, but the eternal
Law enjoins the children of Israel still to celebrate the vintage.
A race that persists in celebrating their vintage, although they
have no fruits to gather, will regain their vineyards.

BENJAMIN DISRAELI

SIMCHAT TORAH

At the very moment we are about to conclude the reading of the Torah, a project that we have worked on relentlessly and religiously for the past year, we grab another Torah scroll and lay it down and, without so much as a pause, start again. *Simchat Torah* means that learning never stops, and it contains one of the fundamental insights of the Jews: "How can I be sad, how can I despair, if there is something more to learn, something more to know?"

LAWRENCE KUSHNER

THE MESSAGE OF CHANUKAH

They were ready either to live or die nobly.

I MACCABEES 4:35

No, *Chanukah* is not the Jewish answer to Christmas. But as far as American Jewish children go—and their parents, too, for that matter—the fact that *Chanukah* comes out in December, lasts for eight full days, and has trappings such as *Chanukah* gelt, gifts, latkes and lots of candles to light doesn't hurt the Diaspora ego one bit.

There are four levels to the story of *Chanukah*, each addressing the Jews of any given generation with a different sense of urgency and immediacy. At one level, it is the story of religious freedom and national sovereignty. At the second, *Chanukah* is about Jewish particularism versus assimilation. The third is a tale of the few against the many, the weak against the mighty and powerful. And the fourth is about lights and miracles.

In the year 167 B.C.E. a small band of Jews—today we would call them guerrillas—took to the hills of Judea. They had had just about all they could take from the Greek oppressors. And besides, they were in mortal danger. But instead of merely hiding safely in the hills they knew so well, they undertook a risky war against the oppressors. It was a war that would bring them, three years later, victorious to the Holy Temple in Jerusalem.

BLU GREENBERG

"THE MENORAH"

Kindle the taper like the steadfast star,
Ablaze on evening's forehead o'er the earth,
And add each night a luster till afar
And eight fold splendor shine above the earth.
Clash, Israel, the cymbals, touch the lyre,
Blow the brass trumpet and the harsh-tongued horn;
Chant psalms of victory till the heart takes fire,
The Maccabean spirit leap new-born.

EMMA LAZARUS

CHANUKAH SONG

Rock of ages, let our song
Praise Your saving power;
You, amid the raging foes,
Were our sheltering tower.
Furious, they assailed us,
But Your arm availed us:
And Your word
Broke their sword
When our own strength failed us.

Children of the Macabees
Whether free or fettered,

Wake the echoes of the songs
Where you may be scattered.
Yours the message cheering,
That the time is nearing
Which shall see
All men free,
Tyrants disappearing.

GUSTAV GOTTHEIL

Passover

Let all who are hungry come in and eat, let all who are needy come in and make Passover.

PASSOVER HAGGADAH

Each year you say that maybe
next year you won't bother
anymore to make the old foods.
The price of fish exorbitant
the $4 a pound becoming 5
two days before the holiday
women bunched together shouting
and then the chopping grating mixing.
Hard work for an old woman.
And nowadays they say the package
is almost as good and cheaper even.

Yet each year
there on that clean ironed white heavy cloth
with its delicate stitches of leaf green
and yellow red—
I hadn't noticed how small the stitch
how intricate the pattern—
the food there again.
Not simple or quick or fancy

but hours of careful shaping.
It is nothing like packaged food.
Nothing.

This year I was
to make tsimes *for another seder.*
We worked together my mother and I
in her kitchen of forty-five years
where the water drips cold
and the hot water never gets
really hot where the oven
must be watched and the
refrigerator strapped closed.
I was to grate 20 carrots.
And I, the jogger, basketball athlete
invested in my woman's body strength
grated 6 carrots with great
difficulty my arm exhausted
my fingers grated.
And you my 4'11"
74 year old mother
grated 14 carrots
without stopping
evenly
not easily or quickly
but calmly
silently
providing again
the dark coarse uneven ground.

BERNICE MENNIS

First of the Four Questions

Man nishtana ha-lay-lah ha-zeh mee-kol ha leilot?
Why is this night different from all other nights?

On all other nights we may eat either leavened or unleavened bread but on this night we eat only unleavened bread.

PASSOVER HAGGADAH

THE FOUR QUESTIONS

I loved the Four Questions and the *afikoman* because these rituals were explicitly reserved to us kids and they were the most consequential events of the evening. Without the Four Questions, the seder could not begin, since the Haggadah provides the answers (and how could one have answers before questions?). And the *seder* could not end unless the children who had "stolen" the *afikoman* were willing to return it for a suitable ransom (in my family, the price was one silver dollar per child), since everyone had to eat a piece of this special "dessert" matzoth before the final grace could be said.

I was the ringleader of the *afikoman* thieves because I had made it my business never to let my father out of my sight. I watched where he put the piece of matzoth that he had wrapped in his napkin and tucked away while trying to distract us with jokes, funny faces, and other diversionary tactics. The instant he left the dining room for the ritual hand washing, I sprang into action, retrieved the special matzoth, and after a quick and raucous consultation with my cousins, rehid it in a new location.

LETTY COTTIN POGREBIN

PRAYER AT THE END OF PASSOVER

For more than 2,000 years the Jewish people, my people, have been dispersed. But wherever they are, wherever Jews are found, every year they have repeated, "Next year in Jerusalem." Now, when I am further than ever from my people, from [my wife] Avital, facing many arduous years of imprisonment, I say, turning to my people, my Avital: Next year in Jerusalem.

NATAN SHARANSKY

PRAYER FOR THE SABBATH BEFORE PURIM

Purim brings to mind the suffering we have endured in many generations. Painful trials and bitter struggles, torments of body and soul have often been our portion. But sustained by the hope that goodness and love would triumph over evil and hate, we have persevered.

Remembering the courage of Esther and the devotion of Mordecai, we give things for the women and men of every age who have helped to keep our people alive . . . although many a bitter experience may await us before prejudice and hate will disappear, still we trust that in the end all humanity will unite in love, knowing that they are one, children all of the Eternal God. Amen.

GATES OF PRAYER

JEWISH HUMOR

Jewish humor plays fast and loose with self-awareness and self-pity, and with the question of when and how exactly we know which is which.

FRANCINE PROSE

Hot chicken soup was the panacea for all illnesses, the elixir of life, the first and last resort. The humble chicken was our family's bluebird of happiness.

One of the classic stories, which has survived to this day, was about the mother who bought two live chickens. When she got home, she discovered that one of the chickens was sick. She did then what any woman with a mother's heart would do—she killed the healthy chicken, made chicken soup, and fed it to the sick chicken.

SAM LEVENSON

There is a Jewish saying that goes: Your health comes first, you can always hang yourself later.

One of my earliest memories as a child is sneezing and having my mother say, *"Zay gezunt,"* which means "You should be healthy." I didn't know that's what it meant. I just knew that was what you said to someone every time they sneezed. I'm still unable, under most circumstances, to refrain from shouting *"Zay gezunt"* in public places. When you're trying to "pass" it can be a dead giveaway.

So I ask myself, "How are issues of health and being Jewish linked? Is it healthy to be Jewish?" And I answer, "Sometimes it is and sometimes it isn't." For example, it's healthy to be happy and to laugh. It's a Jewish tradition to dance, to sing, to laugh and to celebrate. We celebrate births, circumcisions, bar mitzvahs, bas mitzvahs, weddings, anniversaries, birthdays, escaping from Egypt, the beginning of spring, the end of the old year, and every week we celebrate the Sabbath. This is happy and, therefore, one can only assume, healthy.

On the other hand we also suffer a lot. We suffer on our own account and we suffer over the pain of others. Maybe it's because of our history. Who can say? But one thing I can say for sure, we are a people who have suffered. We have suffered social ostracism, religious persecution, poverty, imprisonment, murder, slavery, genocide . . . I could go on and on. Still, as a people we persist—we somehow survive despite the suffering. Despite the illness of the world we still manage to survive.

Some people might say that since we suffer so much and since we manage to survive nonetheless, suffering creates strength and is therefore a positive thing. I think that's false logic. If I had the choice, I'd choose less suffering and take my chances that it would make me less healthy in the long run.

Oy, all this is muddling up my head. But listen, don't worry. Everything will work out, as long as you're healthy. And if not, you can always take the advice Molly Goldberg gave her husband when he came home one cold winter's evening. "Jake," she said, "go take off your coat and hang yourself in the closet."

JUDY FREESPIRIT

IT'S A TRADITION: A JEW ANSWERS A QUESTION WITH A QUESTION

A Jewish insurance broker who sold life insurance policies to alleged members of organized crime . . . was called before a grand jury and when asked "Do you know 'Fat Tony' Salerno?" he responded: "Do *I know* 'Fat Tony'?" The prosecutor pressed him: "Well, do you know 'Fat Tony'?" His answer: "How would I know a man like *that?*" Again he was pressed: "Just answer yes or no. Do you know him?" Again he answered with a question: "What do you mean by 'know'? I know him, but I don't know him. Does that answer your question?" . . . The prosecutor finally gave up.

ALAN DERSHOWITZ

LIBERAL JUDAISM

. . . the enlightenment introduced a whole new dimension to the divisions within the Jewish world. The subsequent political emancipation, which unlocked the ghettos and opened the great universities of Europe, permitted Jews to step outside their ethnic identity and act as individuals. For the first time, Jews had the option of becoming citizens of the wider world without having to convert to Christianity.

In response to this revolution in consciousness, the precursors of the modern Jewish movement—Reform, conservative, and Orthodox—made their debuts. Despite their differences, all three schools of thought faced the same challenge: reconciling the traditions and beliefs of Judaism with modern intellectual and political realities. Out of that dilemma, liberal Judaism—the process of reconsidering and wrestling with traditions, and then self-consciously choosing how to be Jewish—was born.

ANITA DIAMANT

The Jewish Woman: Yesterday and Today

I pray that I may be all that she [my mother] would have been had she lived to an age when women could aspire and achieve and daughters are cherished as much as sons.

RUTH BADER GINSBURG

The experience which made me a feminist was my grandmother's death. I loved her greatly and wanted her to have a *Kaddish*. Since she had no male relative, I asked if I might assume this responsibility. I was told that I could not say kaddish because I was a woman, but that for $350 I could hire a man to say kaddish for her.

RACHEL ADLER

And Deborah Makes Ten

Every year when the day of my father's *yahrzeit* arrives I am faced with the same dilemma. The *minyan* with whom I *daven* on Shabbat does not meet during the week. The local Orthodox synagogue, which has numerous daily *minyans* to accommodate all schedules, makes no provision for women in their chapel. When I do go there the men who occupy the back benches are asked to move up front so that a *mehitzah* can be set up between the men and women—in this case me—

and I can take my place. The process generally elicits grumbles and glares. Neither I nor they are particularly happy with the arrangement. This year I decided to go to the storefront *shul* around the corner from my home. It consists of a group of old men who attend in a devoted fashion. It is a nondenominational mutation of Orthodox and Conservative: a traditional service with mixed seating; women are not counted in the *minyan* or given *aliyot*. Though the sign in front of the *shul* proclaims "BAR/BAS Mitzvahs," once a woman reaches adulthood she does not count.

On the night of the Third of Nisan I took my place among the eleven men gathered for *Ma'ariv*. The rabbi, an elderly retired gentleman with a thick European accent, invited me to sit near him so that he could show me the place. Within a few moments he realized that I was quite familiar with the prayer book and the service. At the conclusion of *Ma'ariv* I asked when *Shaharit*, the morning prayers, would be said. One gentleman answered: "At 8 A.M." Another corrected him: "No, at 7:45." The first man said: "*She* can come at 8:00."

Promptly at 7:45 the next morning I entered the *shul*, I took a prayer book from the shelf and opened it to *Birhot Ha-Shahar*, the morning blessings. Somewhere in the middle of *Pesukei d'Zimra* the gentleman who had decided *I* could come at 8:00 walked over, took the Hebrew/English prayer book I had in my hands and gave me a *Tikkun Mayer*, a prayer book with neither English translations nor instructions. The assumption is that someone who uses this prayer book needs neither. I smiled at him and knew that with that simple act he had just welcomed me into the club. When services ended he looked at me and simply said: "5:45."

At 5:45 that evening I arrived for *Minhah*, the afternoon prayers, feeling good that the day had gone so smoothly. I anticipated being greeted by the strains of *Ashrei*, the psalm which introduces *Minhah*, because the sun was already beginning to set. Instead the room was unnaturally still as the men sat talking quietly. When I walked in they all turned their eyes toward me. The expectant look on their faces and a quick head-count revealed that they were waiting for the ninth and tenth men. I heard the rabbi on the phone trying to find them. "I understand, Mrs. Cohen. No, he shouldn't come out if the doctor told him to stay home. At our age one must be careful." After a few more calls the rabbi announced, "Schwartz is coming." Schwartz would be number nine. We all watched the door, hoping number ten would materialize. I berated myself for not having gone to the Orthodox synagogue, where I would have been guaranteed a *minyan*, even if I had to endure some discomfort.

As they waited for Schwartz to arrive, the president of the *shul* announced, to no one in particular, "In some *shuls* they now count women." A number of men nodded silently. The sun was disappearing and the time for *Minhah* rapidly passing. Finally the door opened and in walked Schwartz. The rabbi glanced at the president and said, "Well, if we are going to say *Minhah* we better start right now." I counted heads to make sure I was right. There was a *minyan*: nine men and one woman.

As *Minhah* ended, I glanced at the clock, knowing that a friend was waiting to take me out for dinner to celebrate my birthday. Even as we remember our losses we go on living and celebrating. And where is it written that you can't laugh and cry on the same day? Reservations had been made for 6:30, and I had solemnly promised that *this* time, unlike previous dinner dates, I would not be late. I knew I could leave right after *Minhah*, for with that service the *yahrzei* ended. As *Ma'ariv* began I was about to leave when I suddenly realized that I had to stay. When I finally arrived at the restaurant I breathlessly explained to my somewhat perturbed friend: "I'm sorry I'm late, but I couldn't leave. I had to stay for *Ma'ariv*."

Then I felt a wonderful wash of warmth and fulfillment fill my body and I smiled a very big smile: "You see, they *needed* me for the minyan."

Yes, they needed me.

DEBORAH E. LIPSTADT

When Women Become Rabbis

The ordination of women will lead to change in (an) important area of Judaism: the way Jews think about God.

As long as the rabbi is a man, a Jew can project the image of the rabbi onto God. But when Jews encounter a rabbi who is a woman, it forces them to think about God as more than male or female. It provokes them to raise questions that most Jews don't like to confront: *What or who is God?* What do I believe about God? That primary religious question leads to others. How can we speak about God? What are the appropriate words, images and symbols?. . . .

All of these questions would lead to a more authentic relationship to Jewish tradition and to God. Once Jews begin to explore their image of God, they will also reevaluate their image of themselves. Because all of us are created in God's image, what we think about God shapes how we think about ourselves. That thinking leads to a reevaluation of men's and women's roles within our tradition and our world.

The ordination of women has brought Judaism to the edge of an important religious revolution. I pray we have the faith to push it over the edge.

LAURA GELLER

Shekhinah

The point is clear. The names of the *Shekhinah* change with the generations, as do the names of every other aspect, male and female, of divinity. God is identified with all of the patriarchs, with all of the heroes, *Shekhinah* is identified with all of the mothers, the heroines of the Bible.

Are we the bride of God, the people whom He weds on that Sabbath of revelation? Are we related to God as female to male, seemingly an image so clear in commentary on the *Song of Songs*? Or are we, as some other imagery seems to say, God's son-in-law, wedded to his daughter the Torah or his daughter the Sabbath? . . . Must we not rather say that we are at once male and female in relating to God, who is Him/Herself at once male and female; both of them inadequate metaphors to describe the mysterious self beyond all gender, indeed, beyond all distinction, but lacking none of the passion we know in our fragile human attempt to unify the polarities?

ARTHUR GREEN

The Highest Goal

Whereas the most desirable goal in secular society may be for women to imitate men, the highest goal for both Jewish men and women is to imitate God. As long as a woman's goal is ultimately to develop herself in order to serve God, not herself, many paths are open to her. This isn't the case for a man, for whom Judaism proposes that he can never fully actualize himself without being married and having children.

From a Jewish perspective, should a woman choose to take on the challenge of having children, her job is not simply to be a "baby machine." Rather, it is to create and mold a Jewish body and soul who will carry on the mandate of perfecting the world in accordance with God's will.

LISA AIKEN

THREE

COMING TO AMERICA

Proclaim liberty throughout the land unto all the inhabitants thereof. . . .

LEVITICUS 25:10

We have had a share in the making of this nation. In the mine and in the mill, at the lathe and at the loom, in counting room and council chamber, the Jew has been at work for two centuries and a half for his America. He has sentried his nation's camp; he has been in the mast's look-out on his nation's ship; he has gone out to battle, and he was among them that fell at the firing line.

Officer, private, whatever his rank, when the nation asked for life or limb, he did not hesitate to offer the sacrifice. In institutions of learning the Jew has made his mark. In the walks of enterprise his individuality has been felt as a telling potency in the development of the greater aims of American energy.

The future will place new solemn obligation upon us for the country's sake and as Judaism's consecration; we shall not shirk our duties.

EMIL G. HIRSCH

THIS CHAPTER RECOUNTS the experiences of the Jewish immigrants who crossed the Atlantic in search of the promise of the New World. There were three separate Jewish waves of immigration to America: the Iberian (Sephardic) of the seventeenth and eighteenth centuries, the Central European of the nineteenth century, and the Eastern European of the late nineteenth and early twentieth centuries. Actually, a very small group came in 1654 at the height of the Spanish Inquisition when Jews were expelled from their homeland. They first went to Portugal and to Holland, and from those two countries many went to Brazil. At one point, a boatload of Jews left South America for a place in the New World called New Amsterdam, which would later become New York City. Here, they were informed that they would have to provide for their own poor, sick, and infirm. And that's when the tradition of Jewish hospitals and community homes began. By the time of the American Revolution in 1776, these Sephardic Jews, although an inconspicuous minority, had become established and accepted members of the New York community.

In the early 1800s, because of the growing anti-Semitism in Europe, Orthodox and Reform Jews from Germany sought a safe haven in the New World. During the last years of the Civil War in 1864, the first immigrants who came from central and western Europe settled in cities along the East Coast like New York, Baltimore, and Philadelphia. Many started as peddlers, selling soft goods on the street from carts. It is believed by some that had it not been for the 2.4 million Eastern European Jews, the Sephardic Jews, now greatly assimilated, would not have been able to sustain a distinct Jewish culture.

But, in New York City, it was not long before the Eastern European immigrants, too, were accepted into society (as much as any non-WASP could be) and began a gradual move uptown. They went into banking and other lucrative fields and soon became philanthropists, engaged in building hospitals and schools.

The Jews of German birth and extraction were just beginning to feel established as Americans when new events occurred, which triggered the newest and largest wave of immigrants to this country. As we all know, the 1800s for the Jews of Russia were not the picturesque scenes of the beautifully crafted stories of Shalom Aleichem. Rather, the czar, desiring to rid the country of its Jews, instituted an anti-Semitic policy that would forever change the face of Russian Jewry. The pogroms of that time took place during the period in Russia after the assassination of Czar Alexander II by members of the revolutionary organization on March 1, 1881. Anti-Jewish circles spread a rumor that the czar had been assassinated by Jews and that the government authorized attacks on them.

Aware of their questionable future, one-third of Russian Jews converted to Christianity, one-third left the country, and a third remained, opting to continue living and hoping for the best. Most of these Jew were killed in pogroms.

Of those who left the country, hundreds of thousands came to the land whose streets were reputedly paved with gold. That so many arrived in a state of decent health was a miracle. It was this overwhelming number of immigrants that gave American Jewry the aggregate it needed to maintain its distinct culture in this foreign land.

This chapter, in a very small way, alludes to the stifling conditions in the steerage of a ship as it steams across the

Atlantic toward the Promised Land. Most of the excerpts concern the conditions that faced the immigrants as they disembarked in New York, but not all of them landed there. Ship captains were encouraged by established East Coast communities to discharge their passengers in ports other than New York, Philadelphia, or Baltimore. Many Jews, bundled in their warm coats, found themselves in strange places like Texas and Louisiana. Hearing of the success of their relatives, other immigrants, some whose last remaining pennies had been sewn into the linings of their clothes, struck out for new, undeveloped areas all over the country. With no money or relatives to meet them, they made homes and new lives for themselves and their families. Whole families worked hard. Small business became large and many earned small fortunes.

Much of what makes American Jewry distinctive today is based on the successes of these immigrants. It was not only their courage to venture across the Atlantic but also their determination to remain and thrive that produced the contemporary Jewish community. One need only to visit the Tenement Museum on the Lower East Side of Manhattan to learn how drastic the conditions were, (sometimes six families shared two small apartments) or read about the loss of children in the face of unrelenting poverty, to understand what real courage was.

The descendants of immigrants faced trials as well—not necessarily of an economic nature. Anti-Semitism has always been a difficult enemy to surmount. But hopefully things are turning around. It may have taken a while, but today the American Jewish population experiences the same freedom under the constitution and the Bill of Rights that is experienced by everyone else in this country. We can be professors and lawyers, CEOs and cinema stars. We are no longer peddlers but owners of most of the private department stores in this country. We not only go to Ivy League colleges, we also head them. (Five of the seven have been headed by Jewish presidents.) We are no longer forced to have our own hospitals, but are the chairmen of departments in every major hospital in America. In other words, no longer is Dr. Rabinowitz compelled to change his name to Dr. Robbins.

It's what our grandparents would have wanted.

*   *   *

THE SHTETL, 1880

The *shtetl* consists . . . of a jumble of wooden houses clustered higgledy-piggledy about a market-place . . . as crowded as a slum . . . The streets . . . are as tortuous as a Talmudic argument. They are bent into question marks and folded into parentheses. They run into culs-de-sac like a theory arrested by a fact; they ooze off into lanes, alleys, back yards . . . [At the center is] the market-place, with its shops, booths, tables, stands, butcher's blocks. Hither come daily, except during the winter, the peasants and peasant women from many miles around, bringing their live-stock and vegetables, their fish and hides, their wagon loads of grain, melons, parsley, radishes, and garlic. They buy, in exchange, the city produce which the Jews import, dry goods, hats, shoes, boots, lamps, oil, spades, mattocks, and shirts. The tumult of the market-place . . . is one of the wonders of the world.

MAURICE SAMUEL

At the peak of its development the *shtetl* was a highly formalized society. It had to be. Living in the shadow of lawlessness, it felt a need to mold its life into lawfulness. It survived by the disciplines of ritual. The 613 mitzvot, or commandments, that a pious Jew must obey, which dictate such things as the precise way in which a chicken is to be slaughtered; the singsong in which the Talmud is to be read; the kinds of food to serve during the Sabbath; the way in which shoes should be put on each morning; the shattering of a glass by the groom during a marriage ceremony—these were the outer signs of an inner discipline.

IRVING HOWE

JOURNEY TO THE PROMISED LAND OF AMERICA

But what said some of us at the end of the long service? Not "May we be next year in Jerusalem": but "Next year—in America!" So there was our promised land, and many faces were turned towards the West. And if the waters of the Atlantic did not part for them, the wanderers rode its bitter flood by a miracle as great as any the rod of Moses ever wrought.

MARY ANTIN

In the evening when we were alone together my mother would make me sit on her footstool, and while her deft fingers manipulated the knitting-needles she would gaze into my eyes as if she tried to absorb enough of me to last her for the coming months of absence. "You will write us, dear?" she kept asking continually. "And if I should die when you are gone, you will remember me in your prayers."

At the moment of departure, when the train drew into the station, she lost control of her feelings. As she embraced me for the last time her sobs became violent and father had to separate us. There was a despair in her way of clinging to me which I could not then understand. I understand it now. I never saw her again.

MARCUS RAVAGE

The boat *British Prince* was like a city floating on water, so great was the number of its passengers. All its passengers were

Russian immigrants; all, save members of our group, were traveling to America as individuals, seeking to improve their position by their own brains and brawn; this one through handiwork, that one through peddling. Members of our group saw themselves as superior to this multitude. "The other passengers are not like us," said we to ourselves, "We are not merely going to America for simple comfort, we are idealists, eager to prove to the world that Jews can work the land!" In our imagination, we already saw ourselves as land-owning farmers dwelling on our plots in the western part of the country. So certain were we that our aims in the new world would be achieved that even on the boat we began to debate which kind of community institutions we would build, which books we would introduce into our library, whether or not we would build a synagogue and so forth. We danced and sang overcome with joyous expectations of what America held in store for us. In spite of seasickness, storms, and tempests which visited us on our journey, we were happy and lighthearted. All the days of our Atlantic voyage were filled with joy.

ALEXANDER HARKAVY

We are huddled together in the steerage literally like cattle— my mother, my sister and I sleeping in the middle tier, people being above us and below us . . . We could not eat the food of the ship, since it was not kosher. We only asked for hot water into which my mother used to put a little brandy and sugar to give it a taste. Towards the end of the [fourteen-day] trip when our bread was beginning to give out we applied to the ship's steward for bread, but the kind he gave us was unbearably soggy. . . .

More than the physical hardships, my imagination was occupied with the terrors of ships colliding, especially when the fog horn blew its plaintive note. . . . One morning we saw a ship passing at what seemed to me a considerable distance,

but our neighbor said that we were lucky, that at night we
escaped a crash only by a hair's breadth.

MORRIS RAPHAEL COHEN

God Called It America

*God built Him a continent of glory and filled it with
    treasures untold;*
*He carpeted it with soft-rolling prairies and columned it with
    thundering mountains;*
*He studded it with sweet-flowing fountains and traced it
    with long winding streams;*
*He planted it with deep-shadowed forests, and filled them
    with song.*
*Then He called unto a thousand peoples and summoned the
    bravest among them.*
*They came from the ends of the earth, each bearing a gift
    and a hope.*
*The glow of adventure was in their eyes, and in their hearts
    the glory of hope.*
And out of the bounty of earth and the labor of men,
Out of the longing of hearts and the prayer of souls,
Out of the memory of ages and the hopes of the world,
*God fashioned a nation in love, blessed it with a purpose
    sublime*
And called it America!

ABBA HILLEL SILVER

Ellis Island: Doorway to the Promised Land

Not like the brazen giant of Greek fame,
With conquering limbs astride from land to land

Here at our sea-washed, sunset gates shall stand
A mighty woman with a torch whose flame
Is the imprisoned lightning, and her name
Mother of exiles. From the beacon-hand
Blows world-wide welcome; her mild eyes command
The air-bridged harbor that twin cities frame.
"Keep ancient lands your storied pomp!" cries she
With silken lips.
"Give me your tired, your poor,
Your huddled masses yearning to breathe free,
The wretched refuse of your teeming shore.
Send these, the homeless, tempest-tossed, to me;
I lift my lamp beside the golden door!"

EMMA LAZARUS

When [the immigrants] finally landed [at Ellis Island], the ground still seemed to sway under their feet as they dragged children and bundles along the walk toward the imposing red brick building. There was more shouting and pushing from guards who made them stand together in groups according to big numbers and the tags tied to their coats.

One by one, groups of thirty people at a time moved slowly forward, through the big door into dark tiled corridors, then— jostling two or three abreast—up a steep flight of stairs. . . .

Although they did not realize it, they were already passing their first test as they hastened down the row in single file. Twenty-five feet away a doctor, in the smart blue uniform of the U.S. Public Health Service, was watching them carefully as they approached him. . . .

ANN NOVOTNEY

Ellis Island. The scene is etched in memory—the long antic-ipated reunion of husband and wife, parents and children, brothers and sisters. The lucky ones, with some money, had been able to emigrate together, and for these, the transition to America would be less disruptive of family life. But the majority could not afford such a luxury. More often, a father or an older brother or sister had left first and sent money home for other family members to join them, sometimes one at a time, like a chain. After months or years of separation they were together again. For many, it was a dream come true, and family life resumed as if no interruption had occurred.

For others, the reunion was a difficult one. Abraham Cahan, in his short story "Yekl," describes the plight of a young immigrant who prided himself on being "a real American." The wife he has reluctantly sent for after three years of separation seems dowdy and unfashionable compared to women he has met in New York. He cannot adjust to her old-country ways, or even to being a husband again, and the marriage ends in divorce.

SIDNEY STAHL WEINBERG

Ellis Island in Russian was called the "Island of Tears," and in every way it merited the name. We all cried. Every immigrant who was sent to the Island spent at least the first day in tears. We cried because of fear and disappointment. We had come a long way: We had sold everything we had and spent every cent, and now we were afraid of being sent back . . . We [had to remain on the island for several days.] We were treated like prisoners with as much sternness and contempt. We marched to bed and we marched to eat our supper; and as we marched, we were counted by people who evidently did not know how to smile. All the way to America, we were scrubbed, cleaned, and examined by physicians and now dirt and squalor seemed everywhere.

RACHEL MITTLESTEIN

SETTLING IN

I was given the privilege of leaving my bundle while I went through the swarming streets to try to find work, as well as a place to sleep, since all the "corners" in the place I had just left were already leased.

The first English expression that struck my foreign ear as I walked through the ghetto that day and which I set down in my American vocabulary were *"sharrap"* (shut up) and *"garrarrehere"* (get out of here). It took me a little while to learn that the English tongue was not restricted to these two terms. . . .

ISRAEL DAVIDSON

The great Western Republic, whose very raison d'être was the freedom these poor Jews were denied at home, in the land of their birth, was not only capable of assimilating a vast immigration, but from the nature of its people and its industries, was an ideal goal for the tenacious, sharp-witted, hard-working Polish Jew. Hence an exodus began from Russia to America, and the Jew, with his never failing adaptability, changed his allegiance from the Eagle to the Stars and Stripes, and his language from Yiddish to Yankee. So that today New York contains a population of upwards of 300,000 Jews—the most Jewish city on the face of the earth.

THE JEWISH YEARBOOK, 1896

I had dreamed of free schools, free colleges, where I could learn to give out my innermost thoughts and feelings to the world. But no sooner did I come off the ship than hunger drove me to the sweat-shop, to become a "hand"—not a brain—not a soul—not a spirit—but just a "hand"—cramped, deadened into a part of a machine—a hand fit only to grasp, not to give.

ANZIA YEZIERSKA

An Architectural History

Tenement buildings on Orchard Street in the heart of Manhattan's Lower East Side stand as living monuments to the history of the Jews in America. By 1900, the second major wave of Jewish immigration had landed more than a half-million very poor Eastern European Jews in New York. Most of them found their way to the Lower East side and the infamous Tenth Ward, which became the most fiercely congested ghetto in America, perhaps in the world. Some blocks had population densities as high as 700 per acre.

Struggling to gain a foothold in this bewildering New World, the new arrivals worked 70 hours a week in the sweat-shops of the garment industry or set off on their own as peddlers. The religious broke *Shabbat* laws and worked in order to eat; they watched their children, schooled on the streets, grow harsh and disrespectful. It was a difficult time in a place that stirred burning homesickness for the green hills of Vilna or the pauperish gentility of the *shtetl*.

But the average stay of Jewish immigrants in the Lower East Side was only 15 years. They moved on—and up—first to Harlem, then to the Bronx and Brooklyn and then across America. Today, only about 30,000 Jews live here—shopkeepers, blue-collar workers, Hebraists, rabbis, teachers and social workers. They live side by side with Chinese, Blacks, Hispanics and yuppies. On Sundays, the Lower East Side is jammed with shoppers, often uptown and suburban Jews, who come back to the earthy street bazaars on Orchard and Canal streets looking for bargains.

DAVID COHEN

AMERICA'S IDEALS

The twentieth century ideals of America have been the ideals of the Jew for more than twenty centuries.

LOUIS D. BRANDEIS

Democracy is always a beckoning goal, not a safe harbor. For freedom is an unremitting endeavor, never a final achievement.

FELIX FRANKFURTER

Hebraic mortar cemented the foundations of our American democracy, and through the windows of the Puritan churches, the New West looked back to the Old East.

OSCAR S. STRAUS

Liberty will not descend to a people. A People must raise themselves to liberty.

FROM THE TOMBSTONE OF EMMA GOLDMAN, DEPORTED ANARCHIST

THE FACTS

. . . Also—and most peculiarly, since we were all supposed to be pulling together to beat the Axis Powers, there were these "race riots," as we children called the hostile nighttime invasions by the boys from Neptune (New Jersey): violence directed against the Jews by youngsters who, as everyone said, could only have learned their hatred from what they heard at home.

Though the riots occurred just twice, for much of one July and August it was deemed unwise for a Jewish child to venture out after supper alone, or even with friends, though nighttime freedom in shorts and sandals was one of Bradley's greatest pleasures for a ten-year-old on vacation from homework and the school year's bedtime hours. The morning after the first riot, a story spread among the kids collecting Popsicle sticks and playing ring-a-liveo on the Lorraine Avenue beach; it was about somebody (whom nobody seemed to know personally) who had been caught before he could get away: the anti-Semites had held him down and pulled his face back and forth across the splintery surface of the boardwalk's weathered planks. This particular horrific detail, whether apocryphal or not—and it needn't necessarily have been—impressed upon me how barbaric was this irrational hatred of families who, as anyone could see, were simply finding in Bradley Beach a little inexpensive relief from the city heat, people just trying to have a quiet good time, bothering no one, except occasionally each other, as when one of the women purportedly expropriated from the icebox, for her family's corn on the cob, somebody else's quarter of a pound of salt butter. If that was as much harm as any of us could do, why make a bloody pulp of a Jewish child's face?

PHILIP ROTH

THE FACTS ABOUT BASEBALL

To the Rabbis who taught in the Jewish parochial schools, baseball was an evil waste of time, a spawn of the potentially assimilationist English portion of the yeshiva day. But to the

students of most of the parochial schools, an inter-league
baseball victory had come to take on only a shade less significance than a top grade in Talmud, for it was the unques-
tioned mark of one's Americanism. . . .

CHAIM POTOK

. . . The solace that my Orthodox grandfather doubtless took
in the familiar leathery odor of the flesh-worn straps of the
old phylacteries in which he wrapped himself each morning,
I derived from the smell of my mitt, which I ritualistically
donned every day to work a little on my pocket. I was an
average playground player, and the mitt's enchantment had to
do less with foolish dreams of becoming a major leaguer, or
even a high school star, than with the bestowal of membership
in a great secular nationalistic church from which nobody had
ever seemed to suggest that Jews should be excluded.

PHILIP ROTH

An American and a Jew

For more than four years now, I have been embarked on a
wondrous, confusing voyage through time and culture. Until
1976, when I was thirty-six, I had always identified myself as
an American Jew. Now I am an American and a Jew. I live
at once in the years 1982 and 5743, (the Jewish year). . . . I
am Paul Cowan, the New York–bred son of Louis Cowan and
Pauline Spiegel Cowan, Chicago-born, very American, very
successful parents; and I am Saul Cohen, the descendant of
rabbis in Germany and Lithuania. I am the grandson of Modie
Spiegel, a mail-order magnate, who was born a Reform Jew,
became a Christian Scientist, and died in his spacious house
in the wealthy gentile suburb of Kenilworth, Illinois, with a
picture of Jesus Christ in his breast pocket; and of Jacob Co-

hen, a used-cement-bag dealer from Chicago, an Orthodox Jew, who lost everything he had—his wife, his son, his business, his self-esteem—except for the superstition-tinged faith that gave moments of structure and meaning to his last, lonely years.

As a child, growing up on Manhattan's East Side, I lived among Jewish WASPs. My father, an only child, had changed his name from Cohen to Cowan when he was twenty-one. He was so guarded about his youth that he never let my brother or sisters or me meet any of his father's relatives. I always thought of myself as a Cowan—the Welsh word for stonecutter—not a Cohen—a member of the Jewish priestly caste. My family celebrated Christmas and always gathered for an Easter dinner of ham and sweet potatoes. At Choate, the Episcopalian prep school to which my parents sent me, I was often stirred by the regal hymns we sang during the mandatory chapel service. In those years, I barely knew what a Passover seder was. I didn't know anyone who practiced archaic customs such as keeping kosher or lighting candles on Friday night. Neither my parents nor I ever mentioned the possibility of a bar mitzvah.

By now, I see the world through two sets of eyes, my American ones and my Jewish ones . . . Even now, as a journalist, I want to be at once a versatile American writer like James Agee or John Dos Passos and an evocative Jewish one like Isaac Bashevis Singer or Chaim Potok. Sometimes it makes me feel deeply conflicted. Sometimes it makes my life seem wonderfully rich and varied. I do know this: that my mind is enfolded like a body in a prayer shawl, by my ancestral past and its increasingly strong hold on my present. Scores of experiences have caused me to re-create myself, to perceive a five-thousand-year-old tradition as a new, precious part of my life.

I am not alone. Indeed, I believe my story, with all its odd, buried, Old World family mysteries, with its poised tension between material wealth and the promise of spiritual wealth, is the story of much of my generation, Jew and gentile alike.

PAUL COWAN

I am an American, an American Jew who, because he is a Jew proudly recalls that on the Independence Bell, which on the 4th day of July, 1776, proclaimed the gladdest tidings that human ears ever hear, there were inscribed the words of the Hebrew Bible, "And ye shall proclaim liberty throughout our land unto all the inhabitants thereof."

STEPHEN S. WISE

Two dynamics are occurring simultaneously among America's six million Jews: continuing and, in many instances, increasing commitments to Jewish concerns (religious education, Israel, Soviet Jewry) by about two-thirds of the group, and flight from virtually all things Jewish by the rest. Will the committed two-thirds succeed in fashioning an authentic American-Jewish civilization, one rich in new forms of individual and communal expression—as did the Jew of Babylonia, who, two thousand years ago, created a host of new Jewish institutions along with the Babylonian Talmud? Or will American Jewry become a modern-day version of the vanished, culturally attenuated Jewry of ancient Alexandria—so much a part of their culture that they finally faded into it?

The future is hidden; the jury still out.

CHAIM POTOK

COMPLETE ACCEPTANCE

Here I am absolutely Jewish. I am appointed to the Supreme Court, and there's already another Jewish member [Ruth

Bader Ginsburg], and there's no issue for or against. My parents and grandparents would never have believed it. It's the kind of ideal that many people have aspired to in terms of the place of a Jew in public life. It's neither a qualification nor a disqualification.

STEPHEN G. BREYER

FOUR

WE REMEMBER THE SIX MILLION

The Holocaust was the state-sponsored systematic persecution and annihilation of European Jewry by Nazi Germany and its many collaborators between 1933 and 1945. Jews were the primary victims—six million were murdered; Gypsies, the handicapped and Poles were also targeted for destruction or decimation for racial, ethnic or national reasons. Millions more, including homosexuals, Jehovah's Witnesses, Soviet prisoners of war and political dissidents, also suffered grievous oppression and death under Nazi tyranny.

OFFICIAL DEFINITION: UNITED STATES HOLOCAUST MEMORIAL

MUSEUM, WASHINGTON, D.C.

We must remind ourselves that the Holocaust was not six million. It was one, plus one, plus one . . .

JUDITH MILLER

MEMORY PERMEATES every part of Jewish history; its life, value stance, and ritual observance. To Jews from antiquity to the present, the concept and reality of "memory" are one. For centuries, Jews have recalled the sorrow at the loss of national identity when the Temple Shrine in Jerusalem was destroyed. We are commanded not only to remember the bondage and deliverance from Egypt, but also to feel the sting of the lash, the torment of a life not our own. On Passover, we tell our children of the days of servitude. We teach them to eat unleavened bread so that they may remember the struggle to be free. We spill wine and think of blood spilled in a hundred Egypts.

In our time, Jews have added another remembrance. Today, we recall the agonies suffered by our ancestors in the Holocaust years. The writer Elie Weisel captured this obsession with memory in his memoir: *Night*.

Never shall I forget that night, the first night in camp, which has turned my life into one long night, seven times cursed and seven times sealed. Never shall I forget that smoke. Never shall I forget the little faces of the children, whose bodies I saw turned into wreaths of smoke beneath a silent blue sky.

Never shall I forget those flames, which consumed my faith forever.

Never shall I forget that nocturnal silence which deprived me, for all eternity, of the desire to live. Never shall I forget those moments, which murdered my God and my soul and turned my dreams to dust. Never shall I forget these things, even if I am condemned to live as long as God himself. Never.

The world is not the same since Auschwitz. The decisions we make, the values we teach and live by must be pondered— not only in the halls of learning but also before the victims of the extermination camps. Along with their descendants, we must never let any of it be forgotten.

Accordingly, Barry Friedman, a contemporary American rabbi, composed a worship service dedicated to the memory of the six million martyrs of the Holocaust. Though each year the survivors diminish in numbers, and the years that separate us from that heinous time increase, still, from the pulpit of his synagogue, Rabbi Friedman speaks these same words:

We cannot permit the world to erase from its mind the memories of Aushwitz-Birkanau, Treblinka and Theresienstadt. Buchenwald is the mark on the forehead of Cain's twentieth century descendants. Lubin-Maidanek and Bergen-Belsen will never happen again only if we sear their names into the conscience of every inhabitant of this planet.

It is the task of the survivors, and we all are survivors, to remind humanity of its inhumanity. We are the reminder that what happened cannot be forgotten. You and I were in Bergen-Belsen. Our eyes mirror Treblinka, our minds are the repository of Maidanek. This service pays tribute to my people who died the martyr's death *al pilkiddush haShem*, for the sanctification of God's name. This service will teach my children that just as they stood at the foot of Sinai with Moses at the decisive moment of Revelation, they also accompanied

Anne Frank into the death camp of Bergen-Belsen. This service is a lesson to my people that *Ahm Yisrael*, the People of
Israel, is one and *Ahm Yisrael Chai*, the People of Israel lives.

Like memory, the wailing does not abate.

*   *   *

HOLOCAUST REMEMBRANCE

Jewish custom prescribes that Holocaust Remembrance Day be marked in the month of April, for it was in April that the Jews of the Warsaw ghetto rose up against their oppressors, with empty hands facing guns and tanks, the most lethal weapons of war.

Come to think of it, though, this is a most unlikely time to mark so somber and melancholy an occasion. After all, April is the first full month of spring, and spring is the time "when the air is calm and pleasant," so Milton wrote, "and it were an injury and sullenness against nature not to go out and see her riches and partake in her rejoicing."

As individuals, we can well do that, we can go out into the public gardens and rejoice, roll up our sleeves to feel a little Springtime warmth; but as Jews, rolled-up sleeves all too quickly remind us of those numbers tattooed on the arms of death camp inmates.

As individuals, we can rejoice in April showers and breathtaking rainbows; but as Jews, we cannot hear of "showers" without shuddering, nor view a rainbow without thinking of the Nazi killers who shattered its radiance, who took its colors and pinned them to our hearts: yellow for Jews . . . red for communists . . . brown for gypsies . . . pink for gays . . . and on and on through the spectrum of murdered souls.

As individuals, we can hearken to the Song of Solomon: "Arise . . . my fair one, come away!" But as Jews, we are mired in agonizing memories and cannot come away. We cannot see a meadow without recalling the poem of a twelve-year-old Jewish inmate of Theresenstadt who said of her captivity that she "never saw another butterfly."

Oh, would that we could forget. But quick forgetting is not the reality of a people for whom nature itself was defiled by the Nazi murderers who sowed bones instead of seeds in the month of April!

ALEXANDER M. SCHINDLER

The six million cannot be named or counted. If each were given one second only, four months would pass, and part of a fifth. We name, instead, the camps and ghettos, those dread places whose very names appall us:

Auschwitz-Birkenau
Bergen-Belsen
Buchenwald
Dachau
Mauthausen
Maidenek
Ponar
Ravensbruck
Treblinka
Theresienstadt
Vilna
Warsaw

The names of the six million belong to God.

BARRY FRIEDMAN, HOLOCAUST MEMORIAL SERVICE

I believe in the sun even when it is not shining.
I believe in love even when not feeling it.
I believe in God even when He is silent.

INSCRIPTION ON THE WALL OF A CELLAR IN COLOGNE,
GERMANY, WHERE JEWS HID FROM THE NAZIS.

GHETTO LIFE 1941–1945

CHRONICLE OF THE LODZ GHETTO, 1941–1944

The chronicle is a document with universal significance: reminiscent of a censored contemporary newspaper, not to be read by anyone except those who wrote it. The chroniclers worked with the facts: viewing people as individuals and as members of families and society in a closed Jewish quarter . . . When the chroniclers sat down to record the events of the day they had no idea what tomorrow might bring. They could not have foreseen, therefore, that the ghetto's post office, literally created out of nothing at great effort, would not be able to send mail, and when, as they note, the ban on mail to the General government was lifted of May 10, 1944, there would no longer be any Jews in that area to receive mail. Neither were the chroniclers able to imagine that the ghetto's orphanages, homes for the aged, and hospitals, whose founding had required such effort, would soon be turned into workshops, and that their inhabitants would be evacuated, "resettled" . . . Indeed, as the Chroniclers themselves noted on July 15, 1944, "The ghetto lost the habit of thinking more than a few hours ahead."

LUCJAN DOBROSZYCKI

Sunday, December 26, 1943.

When something breaks down in the ghetto, it takes a great deal of time and effort to get it working again. "It's a wreck," goes the popular expression. But no one gets too worried about it. The *reboyne sheloylem* will help us out. . . .

Say there's no water in the pipes. A water shortage exacerbates the misery of being in the ghetto. You do what you have to, you go to the well. But since all the tenants need water at the same time, as do our dear neighbors, a *jikehja* forms at once.

Meanwhile, specialists are called in to fix the water pump after the janitor's skill has failed.

Two strapping youths arrive. They examine and study the problem, and then tackle it. Soon you hear the snort of the motor, a noise that heralds the approach of water. A deceptive hope! There are a few drops in the pipe—[and then] the dream is over. The boys have left the scene.

This game is repeated for several days. Is the repair work really so difficult, or is there some other reason for the delay?

Then we learn that a workshop soup kitchen nearby uses the same water pipes. Naturally, our "hydraulics experts" are aware of this. And since they always receive a good *gedakhte* soup gratis whenever they come to do the repairs, they are not in any hurry. Every day, a bit of fixing; every day, a bowl of soup . . .

That's the ghetto. People will take a job for a bowl of soup and walk out on it for another bowl of soup.

OSKAR ROSENFELD

WARSAW GHETTO, SUMMER 1941.

There is music and sound at every step: on the streets, in the courtyards, in the squares. They sing splendid operatic arias, and Polish and Yiddish songs. There are wonderful voices which (have performed) on the concert and operatic stage. . . . Cantors from synagogues large and small, former choristers and ritual butchers sing Hebrew synagogue songs. The ordinary street singers who have no voice and cannot sing, sing strange songs of their own composition.

The same happens with the courtyard music. Real musi-

cians play here: professors from the schools of music and famous violinists from the Philharmonic orchestra and from the
opera. And the most ordinary scraping of violins, plucking of
zithers, and playing of empty bottles can also be heard. This
procession continues through the courtyards from morning
until late at night in spring, summer, and autumn. Most res-
idents show their appreciation and gratitude. Apart from the
theaters and musical cafes, this is how the resident's need for
entertainment is satisfied.

JAN MAWULT

Near the newsstand there is a vendor of candy and cigarettes.
He is an elderly man with the appearance of an intellectual.
He is leaning against the wall, half slumbering. Close by, an
elderly woman at a little table sells arm bands of various qualities, from fifty groszy to two zlotys each. The cheapest are
made of paper with a printed Star of David; the most expen-
sive are of linen with a hand-embroidered Star of David and
rubber bands. These arm bands are very much in demand in
the ghetto because the Germans are very "sensitive" on this
score, and when they notice a Jew wearing a crumpled or dirty
arm band, they beat him at once.

MARY BERG

WARSAW GHETTO, SIMCHAT TORAH, 1942.

Twenty Jews were gathered in the home of Rabbi Menahem
Zemba, the last remaining rabbi in Warsaw, to observe Simchat Torah. Among them was Judah Leib Orlean, former director of the Beth Jacob Teachers' Seminary, who had devoted
his life to religious education. At the proper time they brought
forth the scrolls of the Torah; and, sorrowfully reciting the

verses, which in former years had been joyously chanted, they wearily plodded the *hakafot* about the table.

Suddenly a boy of twelve appeared in the room. This was astonishing, for the Germans had already slain or deported, for extermination, all the Jewish children in the ghetto. Who could he be, and where had he come from? No one knew.

Orlean ran to the boy and, embracing him together with his Torah, cried out, "Young Jew with the holy Torah!" He swept him along in an exultant Hassidic dance. The others joined the dance one by one, until all had formed a circle about the unknown boy, Orlean, and the Torah.

Bereaved fathers who had lost their entire families danced, with tears rolling down their faces, while the great educator reiterated, "Young Jew with the holy Torah! Young Jew with the holy Torah!"

This was the last dance of the last Jews on the last Simchat Torah in Warsaw.

HILLEL SEIDMAN

Out of the five hundred thousand, formerly in the Polish capital, only a handful of Jews remained alive.—ed.

IN THE GHETTO AT THEREZIN: THROUGH CHILDREN'S EYES.

. . . We got used to standing in line at 7 o'clock in the morning, at 12 noon and again at seven o'clock in the evening. We stood in a long queue with a plate in our hand, into which they ladled a little warmed-up water with a salty or a coffee flavor. Or else they gave us a few potatoes. We got used to sleeping without a bed, to saluting every uniform, not to walk on the sidewalks and then again to walk on the sidewalks. We got used to undeserved slaps, blows and executions. We got accustomed to seeing people die in their own excrement, to seeing piled-up coffins full of corpses, to seeing the sick amidst dirt and filth and to seeing the helpless doctors. We got used to it that from time to time, one thousand unhappy souls would come here and that, from time to time, another thousand unhappy souls would go away . . .

PETR FISCHL, FIFTEEN YEARS OLD

"IT ALL DEPENDS ON HOW YOU LOOK AT IT."

Terezin is full of beauty.
It's in your eyes now clear
And through the street the tramp
Of many marching feet I hear.

In the ghetto at Terezin,
It looks that way to me,
Is a square kilometer of earth
Cut off from the world that's free.

Death, after all, claims everyone,
You find it everywhere.
It catches up with even those
Who wear their noses in the air.

The whole, wide world is ruled
With a certain justice, so
That helps perhaps to sweeten
The poor man's pain and woe.

MIROSLAV KOSEK

"THE BUTTERFLY"

The last, the very last,
So richly, brightly, dazzlingly yellow.
Perhaps if the sun's tears would sing
against a white stone . . .

Such, such a yellow
Is carried lightly 'way up high.
It went away I'm sure because it wished to
kiss the world good-bye.

For seven weeks I've lived in here,
Penned up inside this ghetto
But I have found my people here.
The dandelions call to me
And the white chestnut candles in the court.
Only I never saw another butterfly.

That butterfly was the last one.
Butterflies don't live in here,
In the ghetto.

PAVEL FRIEDMANN, TWELVE YEARS OLD

A total of around 15,000 children under the age of 16 passed through Terezin. Of these, around 100 came back.—ed.

JEWISH RESISTANCE

Let the people awaken and fight for its life!
Let every mother be a lioness defending her young!
Let no father stand by and see the blood of his children in silence!

Let not the first act of our destruction be repeated!
An end to despair and lack of faith!
An end to the spirit of slavery amongst us!

CALL FOR RESISTANCE BY THE JEWISH MILITARY
ORGANIZATION IN THE WARSAW GHETTO, JANUARY, 1943

WAITING . . . WAITING

Warsaw, April 29, 1943.

I, Yosl, son of David Rakover of Tarnopol, a Hassid of the
Rabbi of Ger and a descendant of the great, pious and righteous families of Rakober and Meisel, inscribe these lines as
the houses of the Warsaw ghetto go up in flames. The house
I am in is one of the last unburned houses remaining. For
several hours an unusually heavy artillery barrage has been
crashing down on us, and the walls around are disintegrating
under the fire. It will not be long before the house I am in is
transformed, like almost every other house of the ghetto, into
a grave for its defenders. By the dagger-sharp, unusually crim-
son rays of the sun that strike through the small, half-walled-
up window of my room through which we have been shooting
at the enemy day and night, I see that it must be late afternoon, just before sundown, and I cannot regret that this is
the last sun that I shall see. All of our notions and emotions
have been altered. Death, swift and immediate, seems to us
a liberator, sundering our shackles; and beasts of the field in
their freedom and gentleness seem to me to be so lovable and
dear that I feel a deep pain whenever I hear the evil fiends
that lord it over Europe referred to as beasts. It is untrue that
the tyrant who rules Europe now has something of the beast
in him. He is a typical child of modern man; mankind as a

whole spawned him and reared him. He is merely the frankest expression of its innermost, most deeply buried instincts.

ZVI KOLITZ ("YOSL RAKOVER")

This document was purported to have been written by Yosl Ra-kover, a Polish Hasidic Jew. It is, however, a "story" by Zvi Ko-litz, an Israeli Jew who lives in New York and is a teacher at Yeshiva University. The account was so real, it was assumed to be a true document salvaged from the ruins of the ghetto. Even-tually, the work took on a life of its own.—ed.

We have been pointedly reminded that we are in hiding, that we are Jews in chains, chained to one spot, without any rights, but with a thousand duties. We Jews mustn't show our feel-ings, must be brave and strong, must accept all inconven-iences and not grumble, must do what is within our power and trust in God. Sometime this terrible war will be over. Surely the time will come when we are people again, and not just Jews.

Who has inflicted this upon us? Who has made us Jews different from all other people? Who has allowed us to suffer so terribly up till now? It is God that has made us as we are, but it will be God, too, who will raise us up again. If we bear all this suffering and if there are still Jews left, when it is over, then Jews, instead of being doomed, will be held up as an example.

ANNE FRANK

IN THE CAMPS

One day, like people everywhere, six million of our people worked and had children, hoped, made plans, laughed and cried, were foolish or wise, said their prayers, loved, lost, gained, dreamed. One other day they vanished into graves they were forced to dig, or they were turned into ashes that floated upward in eternal reproach of all who breathe.

All these we now remember.

NEW LIGHT SIDDUR, HOLOCAUST MEMORIAL SERVICE

INSIDE TREBLINKA

There was a sign, a small sign, on the station of Treblinka. I don't know if we were at the station or if we didn't go up to the station. On the line over there where we stayed there was a sign, a very small sign, which said "Treblinka." The first time in my life I heard that name "Treblinka." Nobody knew. It was not a place. There was not a city. There is not even a small village. Jewish people always dreamed, and that was part of their life, part of their messianic hope, that some day they're going to be free. That dream was mostly true in the ghetto. Every day, every single night, I dreamed about that. I think that's going to be good. Not only the dream but the hope conserved in a dream.

The day before Succoth, there was a second transport . . . I was together with them. I know in my heart that something is not good, because if they take children, if they take old people, they send them away, that means it is not good. What they said is they take them away to a place where they will be working. But on the other hand, to an old woman, a little child of four weeks or five years, what is work? It was a foolish thing, but still we had no choice—we believed in them.

ABRAHAM BOMBA, SURVIVOR

The "dead season," as it was called, began in February 1943, after the big trainloads came in from Grodno and Bialystok. Absolute quiet. It quieted in late January, February and into

March. Nothing. Not one trainload. The whole camp was empty, and suddenly, everywhere there was hunger . . . And one day *obersharfuherer* Kurt Franz appeared before us and told us: "The trains will be coming in again starting tomorrow." We didn't say anything. We just looked at each other, and each of us thought: "Tomorrow the hunger will end."

The trainloads . . . brought in Jews from Bulgaria, Macedonia. These were rich people; the passenger cars bulged with possessions . . . We threw ourselves on their food. A detail brought a crate full of crackers, another full of jam. They deliberately dropped the crates, falling over each other, filling their mouths with crackers and jam. The trainloads from the Balkans brought us to a terrible realization: We were the workers in the Treblinka factory, and our lives depended on the whole manufacturing process, that is, the slaughtering process at Treblinka.

RICHARD GLAZAR, SURVIVOR

Twenty four thousand people [arrived], probably with not a sick person among them, not an invalid, all healthy and robust! I recall our watching them from our barracks. They were already naked, milling among their baggage. And David—David Bratt—said to me: "Maccabees! The Maccabees have arrived in Treblinka!" Sturdy, physically strong people, unlike the others.

It was staggering for us, these men and women, all splendid, were wholly unaware of what was in store for them. . . .

Beginning in November '42, we'd noticed . . . that we were being "spared." We noticed it and we also learned that Satangl, the commandant, wanted, for efficiency's sake, to hang on to men who were already trained specialists in the various jobs: sorters, corpse-haulers, barbers who cut the women's hair, and so on. This in fact is what later gave us the chance to prepare, to organize the uprising. We had a plan worked out in January 1943, code named "the Time." At a set time we were to attack the SS everywhere, seize their weapons and attack the *Kommandantur*. But we couldn't do it because things were at a standstill in the camp, and because typhus had already broken out.

RICHARD GLAZAR

In Vittel, France

At the station, another girl I saw was about five years old. She fed her younger brother, and he cried. He cried, the little one; he was sick. Into a diluted bit of jam she dipped tiny crusts of bread and skillfully inserted them into his mouth. This my eyes were privileged to see, to see this mother, a mother of five years, feeding her child, to hear her soothing words. My own mother, the best in the world, had not invented such a ruse. But this one wiped his tears with a smile, injecting joy into his heart, this little girl of Israel. Sholem Aleichem could not have improved upon her.

They, the children of Israel, were the first in doom and disaster, most of them without father and mother. They were consumed by frost, starvation and lice. Holy Messiahs, sanctified in pain. Why, in days of doom, are they the first victims of wickedness, the first in the trap of evil, the first to be detained for death, the first to be thrown into the wagons of slaughter? They were thrown into the wagons, the huge wagons, like heaps of refuse, like the ashes of the earth. And they transported them, killed them, exterminated them, without remnant or remembrance.

The best of my children were all wiped out, woe unto me, doom and desolation.

YITZCHAK KATZNELSON

*Katznelson, was murdered in
Auschwitz in 1944 following the murder of his wife and
two younger sons. This poem, hidden in bottles and buried
in the ground in a Nazi concentration camp in Vittel,
France, was discovered after the war.—ed.*

IN AUSCHWITZ

He tried to sleep. Was he right or wrong? Could one sleep here? Was it not dangerous to allow your vigilance to fail, even for a moment, when at any minute death could pounce upon you?

I was thinking of this when I heard the sound of a violin.

The sound of a violin, in this dark shed, where the dead were heaped on the living. What madman could be playing the violin here, at the brink of his own grave? Or was it really an hallucination?

It must have been Juliek.

He played a fragment from Beethoven's concerto. I had never heard sounds so pure. In such a silence.

How had he managed to free himself? To draw his body from under mine without my being aware of it?

It was pitch dark. I could hear only the violin, and it was as though Juliek's soul were the bow. He was playing his life. The whole of his life was gliding on the strings—his lost hopes, his charred past, his extinguished future. He played as he would never play again.

ELIE WIESEL

We Hungarian Jews were better off than the Italian Jews.

The Italians didn't know they were Jewish. I saw a trainload of Italian women come into Auschwitz, after their haircuts after the showers. The Germans took everything away from them as usual, but they left them their high-heeled shoes. In panic, and in rage, they started to fight with one another, using their shoes as weapons. They hurt each other badly. We were better prepared emotionally. This is why we would never have done that—in the boxcars, we shared the cracks of air, we exchanged leaning space, we took turns and helped the sicker and weaker ones. Strangely the anti-Semitism in Hungary prepared us. We had learned that our Judaism was not merely a negative that had caused this horror."

ANNA ORNSTEIN, SURVIVOR

The prisoners inside their barbed-wire universe were not unaware of their total abandonment. They knew themselves excluded, denied by the rest of humanity. In 1940–44 the conspiracy of silence seemed universal. Great Britain shut Palestine's gates, the Swiss accepted only the rich and later the children. "Even if I had been able to sell one million Jews, who would have bought them?" Eichmann asked, not without truth. "What would you expect us to do with one million Jews?" echoed Lord Moyne in Cairo.

There is no one left to count on: this was the feeling that prevailed in Auschwitz, Treblinka and Maidanek. We have been erased from history. Not only men died in Auschwitz but also the idea of man, created in his image. The world burned its heart out there.

ELIE WIESEL

Behind every word I write are ten words I do not write. Night was 864 pages; now it is 120. You think those other 744 pages are not there? They are there. You do not see them.

ELIE WIESEL

WHERE WAS THE REST OF THE WORLD?

I do not think we can exempt any of us, we American Jews. What was our situation? In the first place, it took a long time for us to believe that what was happening was actually true. The Jews in Palestine . . . were much more psychologically prepared to believe what was happening. In addition, the first witnesses were among them. By the time it began to percolate into our minds, we also felt that we were good American citizens and we had to do what the American government wanted us to do, and the last thing the American government wanted was disturbance, uproar, change in immigration quotas, anything they thought would impede the war effort. We did nothing to rock the boat. . . . The Jews in Palestine did rock their boat, and they never worried about it. They had been rocking the British boat for a long time. They were doing it for themselves and out of their enormous sense of national responsibility.

MARIE SIRKIN

Mr. President:

The undersigned scholars and scientists . . . have read that through planned starvation and in slave reservations and through premeditated mass murder, almost two million Jewish men, women and children have already met their death, and that Hitler has now issued an edict calling for the total extermination of the over five million Jews who may still be alive in Nazi-dominated Europe.

We appeal to you to find the means to let every German know what is being perpetrated by his rulers and to warn the German people that for generations this guilt will rest upon them unless the hands of the murderers are stayed.

The letter above accompanied a petition with 283 signatories from over 100 of America's top academic institutions. It was sent to President Roosevelt on March 22, 1943.

RIGHTEOUS GENTILE

Chasiday u-mot ha-olam
  Der unvergessliche Lebenretter [sic] 1200 verfolgter Juden
  EPITAPH ON THE TOMBSTONE OF OSKAR SCHINDLER WHO IS
  BURIED IN THE LATIN CEMETERY OF MOUNT ZION, ISRAEL.
  (THE FIRST LINE IN HEBREW READS *"RIGHTEOUS GENTILE."*
  THE SECOND LINE IN GERMAN READS: *"THE UNFORGETTABLE*
  SAVIOR OF 1,200 *PERSECUTED JEWS."*)

THE JEW WILL BE VICTORIOUS

We are not fighting for ourselves alone in all the great battle-fields to which the Third Reich has summoned us. We are battling for the world's ideals, for the ideals of democracy and liberalism, human peace and cooperation. To battle and even to die for these things is not to make a vain sacrifice . . . Let not Hitlerism, Nazism, achieve the triumph over us of moving us to forswear the things by which and for which our fathers lived. Whatever may be the suffering which Jews must endure in Germany, whatever tortures may be visited upon them, Jews may not, dare not forswear their highest faith and their loftiest ideals. Israel disloyal to itself is Hitlerism triumphant; Israel unimpairably and indeflectibly loyal to its faith in and its power of sacrifice for its divine and eternal ideals is the doom of a thousand Hitlerisms . . .

STEPHEN S. WISE

At War's End: Plight of the Displaced Persons

Classified as "displaced persons," a euphemism for uprooted people, the Jews in occupied Germany thought of themselves not as displaced, but as outcast. Having survived Hitler's murderous cosmos, they had taken shelter in the comfortless climate of his devastated Reich. Now, as inmates of DP (displaced persons) camps, they were suspended between an unspeakable past and an uncertain future, their existence like a time-out of history.

They had still another name, a more exalted one, resonant with the consciousness of their place in Jewish history— *Sheerit ha-Peletah*, a biblical reference to "the remnant that was saved."

LUCY DAWIDOWICZ

I pray that my mother and father may look from heaven and see that their son is Bar Mitzvah today, and may they know that my sister and I have remained good Jews, and will always remain so.

SHMUEL

Shmuel was a thirteen-year-old boy who spoke these words during his improvised bar mitzvah ceremony in a displaced person's camp in Germany shortly after the end of the war.—ed.

Each Day We Look

After liberation from Auschwitz, Isabella Leitner and her sisters Chicha and Rachel took to the road with thousands of other displaced prisoners, struggling to shelter and feed themselves as they searched for relatives and a way to begin their lives again.

Each day, as dusk approaches, we look for deserted homes to sleep in, homes that lodge yesterday's travelers. This kind of life calls for intuition and ingenuity. We have to share, be compassionate, crowd together, grab, run before others get there. . . .

We are helpful and kind to one another. The food we have brought along keeps us well. We keep walking during daylight, settle before dark.

On the third night we find shelter in a room with two large mattresses on the floor. A middle-aged woman joins us to share our "beds." She keeps talking about her twin daughters who were separated from her by Dr. Mengele upon their arrival at Auschwitz. She insists that her daughters are alive. Her faith in their survival is like a religious fervor.

We are skeptical, but we haven't the heart to tell her otherwise. We know that Mengle's particular passion was to perform medical experiments on twins.

We prepare for bed. Rachel and I take one mattress, Chicha and the woman the other. Suddenly, a drunken soldier enters the room. He sizes up the situation and chooses a bed mate . . . selecting Chicha, my dark-haired sister. He quickly undresses and turns out the light.

In the dark the middle-aged woman switches places with Chicha.

In the morning the soldier realizes the deception. He smiles, dresses, and departs. On his way out he tosses a gold watch to his most recent conquest. The woman becomes part of our wandering family.

Finally, we lose her on the road, and much later we learn that she has actually, miraculously, found her twins alive in Budapest.

On our journey the woman never stopped talking about her children. She was certain the gods had decreed that somewhere another mother would give her body to a drunken soldier, as she had done, to save her daughters' virginity. We shall always remember her faith. We do not remember her name.

ISABELLA LEITNER

TRIAL OF KARL ADOLF EICHMANN: FEBRUARY 21, 1961, JERUSALEM

When I stand before you here, Judges of Israel, to lead the Prosecution of Adolph Eichman, I am not standing alone. With me are six million accusers. But they cannot rise to their feet and point an accusing finger towards him who sits in the dock and cry: "I accuse." For their ashes are piled up on the hills of Auschwitz and the fields of Treblinka, and are strewn in the forests of Poland. Their graves are scattered throughout the length and breadth of Europe. Their blood cries out, but their voice is not heard. Therefore, I will be their spokesman and in their name I will unfold the awesome indictment.

GIDION HAUSNER, ATTORNEY-GENERAL OF THE GOVERNMENT

OF ISRAEL

Eichmann's was the only case of capital punishment in the history of the State of Israel.—ed.

THE DANGER LIES IN FORGETTING

"In remembrance lies the secret of redemption."

A QUOTE FROM THE BA'AL SHEM TOV ON THE WALL IN YAD
VASHEM, HOLOCAUST MEMORIAL, JERUSALEM.

The danger lies in forgetting. Forgetting, however, will not affect only the dead. Should it triumph, the ashes of yesterday will cover our hopes for tomorrow.

ELIE WIESEL

What fosters memory of the Holocaust? Essentially, any intellectual tool, any mechanism, any tradition that reduces its abstraction will do so, any way of making individuals and peoples and nations remember that before the Holocaust was a national and international catastrophe, it was a family tragedy, an individual loss. History books and education are important. But my memory of a single infant's leather shoe encased in glass at Yad Vashem in Jerusalem is as powerful.

Abstraction is memory's most ardent enemy. It kills because it encourages distance, and often indifference. We must remind ourselves that the Holocaust was not six million. It was one, plus one, plus one . . . Only in understanding that civilized people must defend the one, by one, by one . . . can the Holocaust, the incomprehensible, be given meaning.

JUDITH MILLER

. . . the present generation stands in a shockingly new relation to Jewish history. It is we who have come after the cataclysm. We, and all the generations to follow are, and will continue to be into eternity, witness generations to the Jewish loss. What was lost in the European cataclysm was not only the Jewish past—the whole life of a civilization—but also a major share of the Jewish future . . . It was not only the intellect of a people in its prime that was excised, but the treasure of a people in its potential.

CYNTHIA OZICK

THE BETRAYAL OF WORDS, THE INADEQUACY OF LANGUAGE

Historians and literary people, trying to keep their distance even as they got close to what they felt was a dangerous subject, helped blur the genocidal aspect of the Holocaust by treating it as the Jewish component in a worldwide landscape of disaster that had no boundaries in time or space. It was fashionable to link Dresden with Auschwitz and to add Hiroshima, Bangladesh, Vietnam and Cambodia, as if all murderous places were interchangeable. In this perspective the concentration camp became a metaphor and Auschwitz a symbol of evil. It seemed less painful to speak of "Life's demonic undertow" or "hell made immanent" than to examine deliberate actions of men and women.

SYLVIA ROTHCHILD

The Holocaust happened to its victims. It did not happen in them. The victims were not the participants. The event swept over them, but they were separate from it. That is why they are "sanctified"—because they did not perform evil . . . And if there is one notion we need to understand more than any other, it is this principle of separation. The people for whom the Holocaust "happened" were the people who made it happen. The perpetrators are the Holocaust; the victims stand apart.

CYNTHIA OZICK

How do you tell children, big and small, that society could lose its mind and start murdering its soul? . . . had we started to speak, we would have found it impossible to stop. Having shed one tear, we would have drowned the human heart.

ELIE WIESEL

SURVIVAL

While working at the Holocaust Museum in Washington, D.C., two years ago, I noticed an elderly woman standing in front of an exhibit of photographs taken of the barracks at Auschwitz. She was a small woman, her hair white and soft. She wore a dress with a flower, her hands clutched the handle of her pocket book in front of her. She stood there, alone. I came up beside her. Sensing I was there, but not turning from the pictures, she began to talk to me. "He did this, young girl," she said. "To so many people . . . my whole family. But not to me . . . Let me show you something, young girl," she said. She opened her pocketbook and reached inside to pull out a white envelope from which she took a photograph. She handed it to me. In the picture, she was sitting on a sofa next to a man with white hair and glasses. Standing behind them, smiling, were thirty or so people, all ages and sizes, some holding babies. "This is how I beat Hitler," she said. "Now you tell me who won."

LEAH TOMASCEWSKY

Jews, don't forget! Write it down! Write everything down. Tell everything that is happening.

SIMON DUBNOW

His last words before being executed by the Nazis in Riga, Latvia, in December 1941. He was eighty-one years old.—ed.

In spite of everything, I still believe that people are really good at heart.

ANNE FRANK

FIVE

TOWARD THE LAND OF MILK AND HONEY

Hear, O Israel

On April 30, [1998] the world will begin to celebrate 50 years of Israeli statehood, 50 short years in which the dreams of millions of Jewish people over almost 6,000 years have taken shape in a small patch of desert. Israel's flourishing is nothing short of a miracle, given the wars with Arab neighbors, the terrorist attacks and the dismissal by world powers.

    Israel officially got its name on May 15, 1948, when David Ben-Gurion, Israel's first prime minister, signed the state's Declaration of Independence in the Tel Aviv Museum of Art, seated beneath a photograph of Theodor Herzl, the Hungarian whose 1896 book, The Jewish State, *laid out the argument for a Jewish homeland. Together with Chaim Weizmann, Israel's first president, and soldier-statesmen like Yitzhak Rabin, the tough hearted Ben-Gurion created a model for Israeli leadership against which the current government can seem like a pale imitation.*

    As Israel marks 50 years, it bears remembering that Israel's friends have often been of the fair-weather variety. During the Holocaust, France and England looked toward the Jewish people with callous—and, in Vichy, France, lethal—disregard. From 1945 until 1948, England stopped its Holocaust survivors from emigrating to the incipient homeland. But Israel, a unique fusion of efficient, modern statehood and ancient faith, has outlasted the cruelties of its detractors.

    As the prospect for peace with Israel's neighbors has become murky of late, it is important not to give up, and indeed, the

Israeli people never have. When Moshe Dayan, as a young soldier with wife and family, first heard the news that the United Nations General Assembly had voted for the establishment of a Jewish state, he wrote, "We were happy that night, and we danced . . . We danced but we knew that ahead of us lay the battlefield."

EDITORIAL, *NEW YORK OBSERVER,* APRIL 1998

I VISITED ISRAEL for the first time four years ago. On the way over, after an hour or two in the air, I walked to the front of the plane near the water cooler to stretch my legs. There I met a woman in her late sixties, an American who had immigrated to Israel fifteen years ago. We started talking and I told her this was my first trip to Israel. "Are you Jewish?" she asked, astonished. I told her I was. "And you've *never* been to Israel? Girlie, you should be *ashamed* of yourself!"

Welcome to the land of milk and honey.

This section, and those that preceded it ("Coming to America," and "We Remember the Six Million") exemplify the modern Jewish Diaspora experience. But it was the antique truths that led to the founding of Israel as a state. At Mount Sinai, over three millennia ago, a covenant was forged between God and a band of newly liberated slaves. From that moment to the present, 150 generations of Jews—from the defenders of Masada to the exiles of Babylon and Rome; from the pogroms of Kishineff to the fires of Auschwitz-Berkenau—have affirmed and reaffirmed the covenant: *We will return to Jerusalem, the city of peace.*

From the time of the destruction of the Second Temple and the resultant exile, there was no immigration to Israel to speak of. The emancipation of the eighteenth century changed the traditional Jewish world by granting Jews a status under the law. But still they experienced the continued persecution by non-Jews around the world. In the 1800s, groups of Jews from Eastern Europe began trickling into Palestine, a place they hoped would grant them a safe haven. These early pioneers constituted small Zionist movements, people all with different agendas. Some were socialists, some religious Jews. Some came "to die in the homeland," others wanted to come because the remnants of the Temple rested there. And some were sparked by the single sentence that closes the Passover seder: *Next year in Jerusalem!*

The first wave of immigrants bought land from the Turks and turned it into collective small farms that later became cities. But it was the bigger wave at the end of the 1800s, defined by the political strivings of Theodor Herzl and others, that resulted in the largest wave of immigration to Palestine. As important as was Moses' wanderings through the desert, the trek of the young idealists who sought to herald the messianic era through Zionism and socialism was just as significant. The *Chalutzim* began to farm the land, pave roads, and build towns and cities. They made deserts bloom, rehabilitated villages and towns, and created a thriving community. Jewish intellectuals revived the Hebrew language. Soon this vibrant Jewish society flourished like the newly planted trees.

Zionism never intended to secure exclusive rights to Israel for Jews. Rather, it has simply fought for the right of Jews to have one place in the world where they can protect each other, where the fate of the Jewish people is not dependent on the beneficence of others. Accordingly, we cannot overlook or underestimate the impact of the Holocaust on the nations of the world and the newly formed United Nations. It proved to Jew and non-Jew alike that only a country of their own would afford the Jew the dignity and protection denied them since the destruction of the Second Temple in 70 C.E.

The world recognized the injustice done to this nation of Jews, and the U.N. and Britain called for the creation of the State of Israel. On May 15, 1948, it became official. On that day, David Ben-Gurion, the provisional Prime Minister of the newly formed State of Israel, stood in the Art Museum of Tel Aviv and declared,

> The land of Israel was the birthplace of the Jewish people. Here their spiritual, religious, and national identity was formed. Here they wrote and gave the world the Bible. After our people was forcibly exiled from its land, the faithful kept watch over her in all the lands of their dispersion; ceaseless were their prayers and hopes to return to their land and there to restore our national freedom.

Today's Israel is undergoing a profound change, a transformation from a society whose first concern is defending itself, to a prosperous progressive one. Everywhere you look you see hints of Israel's national yearnings, the traditions of liberalism and individualism upon which the state was founded. Walk the streets of Tel Aviv today and you will see Ben and Jerry's, McDavid's (McDonald's) and Toys R Us. For a first-time visitor, there is not a hint of the struggles it took to get her where she is today, except perhaps for the predominance of soldiers on the buses, the streets, and in the schools. Yet, when you look at how the country is prospering, it's all the sadder that the return to the homeland has never, not for a minute, been one of peace.

I never saw the woman on the plane again, but by the end of my trip I understood exactly what she meant. Until you've been there yourself, you cannot possibly know the feeling of being in the Jewish homeland. Despite the fact that soldiers are everywhere, you somehow feel, well, safe.

*   *   *

ESSENCE OF ZIONISM

Every Jew living today and every Jew born in the future is really a survivor of the Holocaust. They would not be alive, or born, if Hitler had had his way. We have a special obligation to assure the defeat of Hitler, to assure the existence of the Jewish people, and to assure that the message of the Jewish people will continue to come out of Zion. That can only be achieved here in Israel.

MOSHE ARENS

Deep in the heart of every Jew, in its purest and holiest recesses, there blazes the fire of Israel.

ABRAHAM ISAAC KOOK

Zionism is a dream that cannot fail to move and thrill anybody who knows anything of the tragic history of the Jews. The images of Jews dispersed and persecuted, and then the images of miraculous return and revival, can only lead to admiration and joy. A people afflicted and punished for 2,000 years is coming back to its ancient homeland, to turn its ruins and wastes into a thriving garden which will serve as a safe haven.

BENJAMIN BEIT-HALLAHMI

Dr. Chaim Weizmann was lobbying British politicians to win their support for the Zionist effort to gain a Jewish homeland. One member of the House of Lords said to him, "Why do you Jews insist on Palestine when there are so many undeveloped countries you could settle in more conveniently?" Weizmann answered, "That is like my asking you why you drove twenty miles to visit your mother last Sunday when there are so many old ladies living on your street."

HAROLD KUSHNER

Ever since I learned Zionism from Ze'ev Binyamin Herzl and Ze'ev Jabotinsky, I believe with all my heart that *Eretz Israel* belongs to the whole Jewish people and not only to those Jews who live in it. Hence, I have no objection to Jews who live in the Diaspora criticizing the policy of the Israel government of the day; by its very democratic nature, it is transient.

MENACHEM BEGIN

To You Who Dwell in the Diaspora

Being an American Jew (or a Jew anywhere outside Israel) gives one the right to participate in the Israeli political decision-making process—but *only* if one exercises that right by becoming an Israeli citizen and moving to Israel. A Jew who does not make *Aliyah* does not have a direct vote in Israel's future. We may support, cheer, contribute to, defend, invest in, send our children to, pray for, criticize, even love the Jewish state, but the Israeli democracy is composed of 4.5 million Jews, and nearly a million Arabs and others. The citizens of Israel must decide its future.

ALAN DERSHOWITZ

The tourist in Israel is startled by the *Jewishness* of it all. On my first night in Tel Aviv I felt . . . amazement . . . as I saw Hebrew signs on every store-front, Hebrew letters on traffic signals, Hebrew menus posted outside every restaurant. It seemed incredible to me that everyone hurrying across the street at one busy intersection should be Jewish, and the children tossing a ball should cry out to one another in Hebrew.

In the United States . . . Jews learn to make themselves inconspicuous; it is a reflex, an exaggerated reaction to the fear of anti-Semitism, perhaps. A Jew remembers that he is Jewish, and therefore somehow different from most of the other people on the street.

In Israel, where Jewishness is universal, the American Jewish tourist . . . does not need to feel like an alien. In Tel Aviv it is the *goy* who is the alien. The Jew does not have to make, here, the little explanations that he was always making in the United States.

ROBERT SILVERBERG

The people of Israel were exiled from their land, but their land was never exiled from their hearts. In whatever country they dwelt throughout the nineteen Diaspora centuries, they yearned for their homeland, Israel.

MOSHE DAYAN

IN SEARCH OF THE JEWISH STATE

Im tirzu, ein zoh aggadah
   If you will it, it is not a dream.

THEODOR HERZL, 1896

The whole plan is in its essence perfectly simple, as it must necessarily be if it is to come within the comprehension of all. Let the sovereignty be granted us over a portion of the land large enough to satisfy the reasonable requirements of a nation; the rest we shall manage for ourselves.

The creation of a new state is neither ridiculous nor impossible. . . . The government of all countries scourged by anti-Semitism will serve their own interest in assisting us to obtain the sovereignty we want . . . The departure of the Jews will be . . . gradual and continuous, and will cover many decades. The poorest will go first to cultivate the soil. In accordance with a preconcerted plan, they will construct roads, bridges, railways and telegraphs, regulate rivers and build their own habitation; their labor will create trade, their trade will create markets, and markets will attract new settlers; for every man will go voluntarily, at his own expense and at his own risk. The labor expended on the land will enhance its value, and the Jew will soon perceive that a new and permanent sphere of operation is opening here for that spirit of enterprise which has heretofore met only with hatred and obloquy.

And what glory awaits those who fight unselfishly for the course!

Let me repeat once more my opening words: The Jews wish to have a state, and they shall have one. We shall live at last as free men on our own soil, and die peacefully in our own home. The world will be fed by our liberty, enriched by our wealth, magnified by our greatness. And whatever we attempt there to accomplish for our own welfare will react with beneficent force for the good of humanity.

THEODOR HERZL, SEPTEMBER 3, 1897

The speech above was given at the convocation of the First Zion Organization in Basel, Switzerland. Later that night Herzl wrote in his diary . . . "Today, at Basel, I founded the Jewish State. If

*I said this out loud today, I would be greeted with universal
laughter. In five years perhaps, and certainly in fifty years, everyone will realize it . . ."*

*Precisely fifty years and nine months later, the State of Israel
was proclaimed—ed.*

ISRAEL, AT LAST, ISRAEL

MY FATHER'S TEARS: NOVEMBER 29, 1947

The whole neighborhood had maybe one radio set, and
people crowded around it to hear the transmission from the
United Nations General Assembly. . . . Because of the time
difference, the vote on partition started at nine or ten in the
evening, Jerusalem time. I went to sleep and woke up to loud
cries from the street. My father took me outside. People were
shouting and singing. . . . Strangers were hugging and kissing
with tears in their eyes.

About two o'clock in the morning, my father brought me
back home and put me to bed. Then he climbed in beside
me, still in his clothes—something he never did. In the pitch
dark, he told me stories of how he'd been abused by anti-
Semites back in Vilna in his youth, and at school and university.

I remember him explaining to me that I might still be bullied
in school, but not for being Jewish. This was the significance of
the Jewish state. And I saw—well, I didn't really see, because it
was so dark—but rather I sensed tears on his face. It was the
first and probably the only time I saw my father cry.

AMOS OZ

They knew the sound. For months before this afternoon . . .
the forlorn wail had symbolized the frontiers of their existence.

It was the skirl of British bagpipes, and now its call reverberated for the last time down these ancient stone passageways, piping away the few British soldiers left inside the old walled city of Jerusalem. They marched in columns, silent and unsmiling, the rhythmic tramp of their boots blending with the dying notes of the bagpipes. At the head and the rear of each column one soldier, a Sten gun crooked in his elbow, broke the pattern of their unwavering stares, his restless eyes scanning the hostile stone facades around them.

Along the Street of the Jews, from the sculptured stone windows of their synagogues and the mildewed hallways of their sacred houses of learning, the bearded old men watched them go. Their ancestors had watched other soldiers march out of Jerusalem: Babylonians, Assyrians, Romans, Persians, Arabs, Crusaders and Turks, the martial predecessors of these departing British soldiers whose brief thirty-year reign over Jerusalem was now ending. Rabbis, Talmudic scholars, interpreters of the Law, pale and stooped from years of unremitting study, those old men and their forebears had huddled for centuries under the walls of Jerusalem, a forgotten fragment of Jewry, living on the charity of their scattered brethren, caretakers of the Jewish heritage of the City of David. They had kept the Sabbath and conformed every action of their poor lives to the precise prescriptions of the Law. They had memorized their Torah verses and painstakingly copied down the Talmudic texts they passed from generation to generation. And daily they had bowed before the stones of the Temple Mount, beseeching the God of Abraham to bring His people back one day to the Land of Zion from which they had been cast.

That day had never been so close.

LARRY COLLINS AND DOMINICK LA PIERRE

On May 14, 1948, the State of Israel was established. On February 14, 1949, Israel's first parliament was convened in Jeru-

*salem. It adopted the traditional Hebrew name, Kneset. On
February 17, 1949, in front of the Kneset and a waiting world,
Chaim Weizmann was sworn in as President of Israel. This ex-
cerpt is from his inaugural address—ed.*

And now it has fallen to our generation to cement anew the
links of that life of freedom that were snapped by tyranny's
force nearly 1,900 years ago. I do not know why it is precisely
our generation that has been privileged to bring about what
many generations before us longed for in the exiles of darkness. Unless we earned it by all the hardships, weariness,
sorrow and tribulation that have been our portion during the
past seventy years, when one-third of our nation was annihi-
lated.

We suffered torture and affliction as no other nation in the
world and because we are a remnant—and no more than a
remnant—double and treble responsibility lies upon us to fill
the terrible void in our national life.

The world is watching us now to see which way we choose
for ourselves in ordering our lives, and is listening to hear
whether a new message will go forth from Zion, and what that
message will be.

This day is a great day in our lives. Let us not be over
arrogant if we say that this is a great day in the history of
the world. In this hour a message of hope and good cheer
goes forth from this place in the sacred city to all oppressed people and to all who are struggling for freedom and
equality.

CHAIM WEIZMANN

*If I forget thee, O Jerusalem, let my right hand forget
her cunning.*

*If I do not remember thee, let my tongue cleave to the
roof of my mouth; if I prefer not Jerusalem above
my highest joys.*

PSALMS 137:5–6, SONG OF THE EXILED CHILDREN OF
ISRAEL, SUNG BY THE WATERS OF BABYLON.

ISRAEL'S PLACE IN HISTORY

We have always been a small people numerically and we
shall remain a small people, unable to compete with our
rivals in population, territory, natural resources and strength
of armed forces. But the place of our country in the world
cannot be measured in quantitative terms. Few people
have had so profound an influence upon so large a part of
the human race. And there are few countries which have
played so central a role in world history as the land of Israel.

DAVID BEN-GURION

The story of this little sect—the most remarkable survival of
the fittest known to humanity—in no way corresponds with
its numbers; it is not a tale of majorities. It is a story that has
chapters in every country on earth, that has borne the impress
of every period. All men and all ages pass through it in unending procession.

ISRAEL ZANGWILL

Why is Israel compared to a dove?
    All other birds, when tired, rest upon a rock or upon the
branch of a tree. Not so the dove. When the dove tires, she does
not cease flying; she rests one wing and flies with the other.

BERESHIT RABBAH, 39:10

THE JEWISH HOMELAND

The world is divided into places where [the Jews] cannot live, and places into which they cannot enter.

CHAIM WEIZMANN

The difference between little Palestine and bigger, richer countries is one and one only. In other countries there is room for a definite number of Jews. But ask any Jew in Palestine, "What do you lack?" and the answer will be: "More immigration! More! More! More!"

CHAIM WEIZMANN

HATIKVAH: THE ISRAELI NATIONAL ANTHEM

Kol od ba-levav p'nimah
Nefesh y'hudi homiyah
U-l'fa-atei mizrah kadimah
Ayin l'Tziyon tzofiyah
Od lo avdah tikvatenu
Ha-tikfvah bat sh'not alpayim
Li-h'yot am hofshi b'artzenu
Eretz Tziyon vi-ruhalayim.

As long as the heart of the Jew beats,
And as long as the eyes of the Jew look eastward,
Then our two-thousand-year hope is not lost,
To be a free nation in Zion, in Jerusalem.

NAFTALI HERZ IMBER

FIGHTING FOR FREEDOM

May 1, 1956

Let us not recoil from seeing the hate which fills the lives of hundreds of thousands of Arabs surrounding us. Let us not turn away our eyes, lest our hand weakens. This is our generation's fate. Our choice—to be ready and armed, strong and tough, for if the sword loosened from our fist, our lives will be felled.

MOISHE DAYAN, CHIEF OF STAFF OF THE ISRAEL DEFENSE FORCES, *FROM THE EULOGY FOR ROY ROTBERG, KILLED BY ARABS ON THE GAZA BORDER.*

June 5, 1967, marked a watershed in contemporary Jewish affairs. The Six Day War united the members of the generations that witnessed the founding of the State with those of a new generation, one that grew up accepting the existence of Israel as a matter of fact, only to encounter suddenly the harsh possibility of its destruction, making both generations deeply aware of the shared fate of all Jews, and the way that fate is now bound up with the political entity that is the State of Israel.

DANIEL ELAZAR

I have given instructions that I be informed every time one of our soldiers is killed, even if it is in the middle of the night. When President Nasser leaves instructions that he be awakened in the middle of the night if an Egyptian soldier is killed, there will be peace.

GOLDA MEIR

I dislike the Arabs more for making killers out of my sons than for killing my sons.

GOLDA MEIR

The night is still.
The autumn birds doze in the warm air.
The prayers of evening done,
now workers sleep, villages slumber,
At first light of dawn,
the noise of engines from the east, and
the tanks—their flat and ugly roar.
Yom Kippur morning to the east.
and the tanks slowly roar toward the west.
Where are our children, where our fathers?
What has happened to my beloved?
All alike they ask it,
of the night so silent and still.

NEW LIGHT SIDDUR

The little park planted in the memory of a boy
who fell in the war begins
to resemble him
as he was twenty-nine years ago.
Year by year they look more alike.
His old parents come almost daily
To sit on a bench
And look at him.

And every night the memory in the garden
Hums like a little motor:
During the day, you can't hear it.

YEHUDI AMACHI

ENOUGH OF BLOOD AND TEARS

The White House, September 13, 1993
This signing of the Israeli-Palestinian declaration of principle here today—it's not so easy—neither for myself as a soldier in Israel's wars nor for the people of Israel, nor to the Jewish people in the Diaspora, who are watching us now with great hope mixed with apprehension. It is certainly not easy for the families of the victims of the war's violence, terror, whose pain will never heal . . . For them this ceremony has come too late.

YITZHAK RABIN,
AT THE ISRAELI-PALESTINEAN PEACE ACCORD SIGNING

Let me say to you, the Palestinians, we are destined to live together on the same soil in the same land. We, the soldiers who have returned from battles stained with blood; we who have seen our relatives and friends killed before our eyes; we who have attended their funerals and cannot look in the eyes of their parents; we who have come from a land where parents bury their children; we who have fought against you, the Palestinians—we say to you today, in a loud and clear voice: enough of blood and tears. Enough!

YITZHAK RABIN

SEARCHING FOR PEACE

I have no illusions that peace can be achieved rapidly, but I have every confidence that it is going to be possible to inch toward it, inch by agonizing inch.

ARTHUR J. GOLDBERG

A JEWISH CHILD PRAYS FOR PEACE

What shall I ask You for, God?
I have everything
There's nothing I lack.
I ask only for one thing
And not for myself alone;
It's for many mothers, and children, and fathers—
Not just in this land, but in many lands hostile to each other
I'd like to ask for Peace.
Yes, it's Peace I want,
And You, You won't deny the single wish of a girl.
You created the Land of Peace,
Where stands the City of Peace,
Where stood the Temple of Peace,
But where still there is no Peace . . .

What shall I ask You for, God? I have everything.
Peace is what I ask for,
Only Peace.

SHLOMIT GROSSBERG, AGE THIRTEEN, JERUSALEM

AN ARAB CHILD DOES, TOO

In my dream, O mother mine,
I saw an angel with wings pure white
Breaking the rifles one by one,
Shattering to pieces each gun,
Which then into the fire he dashes
And turns into smoldering ashes.

In my dream, O mother mine,
I saw an angel with wings pure white
Scattering the ashes clean
Over the glittering scene.

And the ashes turning into a white dove,
Hovering over the East, jubilant above.

In my dream, O mother mine,
I saw an angel with wings pure white
Lifting Moses and Mohammed up to the skies
And demanding they shake hands and be wise.
I heard his voice thunder and echo after them:

Quick, make haste, O sons of Shem—
Behold he is coming, the herald of Peace.
Singing a song of praise to Peace.

GASSOUB SERHAN, AGE FOURTEEN, KFAR YAFIA
(ARAB VILLAGE)

Prayers of the Parents

An Arab shepherd is searching for his goat on Mount Zion
And on the opposite mountain I am searching
For my little boy.
An Arab shepherd and a Jewish father
Both in their temporary failure.
Our voices meet
About the Sultan's Pool in the valley between us.
Neither of us wants
The child or the goat to get caught in the wheels
Of the terrible Had Gadya machine.
Afterward we found them among the bushes
And our voices came back inside us, laughing and crying.
Searching for a goat or a son
Has always been the beginning of a new relation in these
  mountains.

YEHUDA AMACHI

A Prayer for All

> Stop looking through the rifle-sights
> And lift your eyes in hope.
> A song of love and not of war,
> The song we'll sing is here
> don't say the day of peace will come,
> Bring it by your work.

YAHACOB ROTBLIT

The Art of the Jewish People

Never was this people stronger than [in] its moment of weakness, never more hopeful than in its hour of despair.

ABBA EBAN

In February, 1962, Hadassah Medical Center in Jerusalem celebrated the dedication of the stained glass windows created for the Center's synagogue by Marc Chagall. Chagall delivered a speech at this dedication, of which the following are excerpts:

How is it that the air and earth of Vitebsk, my birthplace, and of thousands of years of exile, find themselves mingled in the air and earth of Jerusalem?

How could I have thought that not only my hands with their colors would direct me in my work, but that the poor hands of my parents and of others and still others, with their mute lips and their closed eyes, gathered and whispered behind me, would direct me as if they also wished to take part in my life?

I feel, too, as though the tragic and heroic resistance movements, in the ghettos, and your war here in this country, are blended in my flowers and beasts and my fiery colors . . .

The more our age refuses to see the full face of the universe and restricts itself to the sight of a tiny fraction of its skin, the more anxious I become when I consider the universe in its eternal rhythm, and the more I wish to oppose the general current.

Do I speak like this because, with the advance of life, the outlines surrounding us become clearer and the horizon appears in a more tragic glow?

I feel as if colors and lines flow like tears from my eyes, though I do not weep. And do not think that I speak like this from weakness—on the contrary, as I advance in years the more certain I am of what I want, and the more certain I am of what I say.

I have concluded two years of labor, creating these twelve stained glass windows for this synagogue in Jerusalem. My hope is that the synagogue will please you and that it will overflow with harmony even as I have prayed.

I saw the hills of Sodom and the Negev, out of whose defiles appear the shadows of our prophets in their yellow garments, the color of dry bread. I heard their ancient words.

Have they not truly and justly shown in their words how to behave on this earth and by what ideal to live?

MARC CHAGALL

When I came to this country in 1921, its Jewish population amounted to 80,000, and the entry of each Jew depended on permission granted by the mandatory government. We are now [1975] a population over 3,000,000 of whom more than 1,000,000 are Jews who have arrived since the establishment of the state under Israel's Law of Return, a law that guarantee's the right of every Jew to settle here. I am also grateful that I live in a country whose people have learned how to go on living in a sea of hatred without hating those who want to destroy them and without abandoning their own vision of peace. To have learned this is a great art, the prescription for which is not written down anywhere. It is part of our way of life in Israel.

GOLDA MEIR

Looking Back

If history remembers me at all, in any way, I hope it will be as a man who loved the Land of Israel and watched over it in every way he could, all his life.

YITZHAK SHAMIR

Looking back, I think we were too sure of ourselves, believing that once we had a nation we could change the world. Now, I'm not so certain. It seemed then as if the sacrifices were worth it for the sake of future generations, but many generations have passed and there's still no peace. I think that most of the Independence War was a miracle, although I don't believe in miracles.

RACHEL OGEN

Petitions of Our Hearts

Memorial service for fallen soldier eitan gissen, age twenty

What do we ask, O God? Are the petitions of our hearts so great, so demanding?

We ask that children spend their nights above the ground, and not in bunkers, that the sounds echoing in the valley are those of birds and not mortars. That roads be built for cars and not tanks. That airplanes be used to carry families on vacation and not to destroy cities.

We ask that prayers not be interrupted and lives destroyed. We ask that the young grow straight and the old see contentment in their grandchildren.

The fields of war are for the moment quiet. The sun moves closer to the horizon and quiet reigns. If the world would appreciate this stillness and end war, leave youth to its dreams and allow them to create positively, freely and with love. If the world would leave youth to its love; love of man for woman, brother for brother . . . then nation would not lift up sword against nation and they would not learn war anymore.

Oh God, let us put aside our weapons and take up the book and the plough.

Ten lanu shalom—give us peace.

BARRY FRIEDMAN

What you do know is that there is one fact of Jewish life unchanged by the creation of a Jewish state: you cannot take your right to live for granted.

SAUL BELLOW

A FINAL PLEA

I wish to thank each and every one of you, who have come here today to take a stand against violence and for peace. This government, which I am privileged to head, together with my friend Shimon Peres, decided to give peace a chance—a peace that will solve most of Israel's problems.

I was a military man for 27 years. I fought as long as there was no chance for peace. I believe that there is now a chance for peace, a great chance. We must take advantage of it for the sake of those standing here, and for those who are not here—and they are many.

Violence erodes the basis of Israeli democracy. It must be condemned and isolated.

This is not the way of the State of Israel. In a democracy there can be differences, but the final decision will be taken in democratic elections, as the 1992 elections which gave us the mandate to do what we are doing, and to continue on this course.

I want to say that I am proud of the fact that representatives of the countries with whom we are living in peace are present with us here, and will continue to be here: Egypt, Jordan and Morocco, which opened the road to peace for us. I want to thank the President of Egypt, the King of Jordan, and the King of Morocco, represented here today, for their partnership with us in our march towards peace.

But more than anything, in the more than three years of this Government's existence, the Israeli people has proven that it is possible to make peace, that peace opens the door to a better economy and society; that peace is not just a prayer.

The path of peace is preferable to the path of war. I say this to you as one who was a military man, someone who is today Minister of Defense and sees the pain of the families of the IDF soldiers. For them, for our children, in my case for our grandchildren, I want this Government to exhaust every opening, every possibility, to promote and achieve a comprehensive peace.

This rally must send a message to the Israeli people, to the Jewish people around the world, to the many people in the Arab world, and indeed to the entire world, that the Israeli people want peace, support peace.

For this, I thank you.

YITZHAK RABIN, NOVEMBER 4, 1995, PEACE RALLY,
TEL AVIV, CITY HALL PLAZA

Minutes after the rally ended, Rabin was shot and killed by Yigal Amir, a Jewish extremist.

SONG OF PEACE

Let the sun rise, the morning shine,
The most righteous prayer will not bring us back.
Who is the one whose light has been extinguished
And buried in the earth?
Bitter tears will not wake him, will not bring him back.
No song of praise or victory will avail us.
Therefore, sing only a song of peace.
Don't whisper a prayer—
sing aloud a song of peace.

—YAHACOB ROTBLIT

Prime Minister Yitzhak Rabin sang this song with over 100,000 people at the Peace Rally in Tel Aviv minutes before his assassination. The words were read by Prime Minister Shimon Peres at the state funeral for the fallen leader.—ed.

SIX

As Others See Us

If the statistics are right, the Jews constitute but one percent of the human race. It suggests a nebulous dim puff of star dust lost in the blaze of the Milky Way. Properly the Jew ought hardly to be heard of; but he is heard of, has always been heard of. He is as prominent on the planet as any other people, and his commercial importance is extravagantly out of proportion to the smallness of his bulk. His contributions to the world's list of great names in literature, science, art, music, finance, medicine, and abstruse learning are also way out of proportion to the weakness of his numbers. He has made a marvelous fight in this world, in all the ages; and has done it with his hands tied behind him. He could be vain of himself, and be excused for it. The Egyptian, the Babylonian, and the Persian rose, filled the planet with sound and splendor, then faded to dream-stuff and passed away; the Greek and the Roman followed, and made a vast noise, and they are gone; other peoples have sprung up and held their torch high for a time, but it burned out, and they sit in twilight now, or have vanished. The Jew saw them all, beat them all, and is now what he always was, exhibiting no decadence, no infirmities of age, no weakening of his parts, no slowing of his energies, no dulling of his alert and aggressive mind. All things are mortal but the Jew; all other forces pass, but he remains. What is the secret of his immortality?

MARK TWAIN

As long as they were locked in the ghetto, isolated socially in the *shtetls*, barred from owning land or pursuing a multitude of professions, businesses, or crafts, the Jew was "spared" the concern of what others thought of him or her. But that did not mean that such antipathy and repugnance did not exist. Those of my generation were taught in elementary school that religious freedom was practiced in the New World. But to the early colonists, who fled religious persecution, Jews were still perceived as heathens who had yet to see the light. Even William Penn—founder of Philadelphia, the city of Brotherly Love—implored Jews to recognize the "error of their ways," and accept Jesus.

For years, Jews have wandered the globe to escape persecution. As early as the fifteenth century when they were sent from their home in Spain, those who attempted to start a new beginning in America were turned back. Five hundred years later, the story was the same.

The rise of Nazism and the Nazi Party manifested a modern appearance of government-sponsored anti-Semitism. A Nazi decree of March 15, 1938, declared that "A Jewish half-bred descended from two full-blooded Jewish grandparents, is considered a Jew." The silence of the world to these decrees, Nuremberg laws, *Kristallnacht*, and the atrocities that followed in predictable procession isolated the Jew as never before.

But after World War II, as the frightful facts of the Holocaust became known and a Jewish State was established, most

Jews were recipients of sympathy, admiration, and respect. The American experience soon became one of acculturation and homogenization. Soon, most Jews felt comfortable enough to leave the "old ethnic" neighborhood. Today, they have entered into business, professional, and social relationships with their Christian neighbors.

Clearly there are still some small pockets of anti-Semitism throughout the county. Synagogues are still burned, hate crimes persist. But inter-religious communities come together in the face of these incidents as never before. Not that long ago, after the desecration of a synagogue in a small American city, a candlelight parade took place through the streets where each person in the predominately non-Jewish community walked, carrying a candle-lit menorah, down Main Street.

There are many reasons for the sharp decline of anti-Semitism in America but a significant one reflects the changing character of doctrinaire Christianity and Church leadership. At the helm of the Christian doctrine is the Pope. "I am convinced," Pope John Paul II said, "and I am happy to state it on this occasion, that the relationships between Jews and Christians have radically improved in these years. Where there was ignorance and therefore prejudice and stereotypes, there is now growing mutual knowledge, appreciation, and respect. There is, above all, love between us. . . ."

This section reflects the evolution of the non-Jewish majority's relations and feelings towards Jews and Judaism. It contains public declarations of Christians concerning the dream of a national Jewish homeland; how they view anti-Semitism and discrimination. The appearance of a Jewish presence in Ivy League academia, hospitals, banks, corporations, and certain professions that were virtually closed to Jews in the past, and the acceptance of Jews into the social lives of Christians, expresses as much about America and the world as it does about Jews and Christians.

You will notice I have selected only positive passages to

include in this chapter, although you can imagine the number of anti-Semitic declarations I came across in my research. They are everywhere. So, despite the fact that it may seem imbalanced, as the editor of this book it is my decision not to provide a forum for words I consider to be meaningless, if not hateful. Why would I?

While working on a different book several years ago, I visited a small town in the Midwest, Corydon, Iowa. Population: 1,724. No Jews. On the evening of the day I arrived, my host invited ten members of the community to his home to have dinner with me. As we sat around the dinner table finishing our coffee, my host brought up the subject of his new car. With great pride, he allowed as how he managed to buy it at a rock-bottom price by *"Jewing-down"* the salesman. What to do? My choices: be polite and let it pass, call him on the slur, or try to educate this man who had, by his own admission, never before known a Jew. Of course, he realized immediately what he had said, explaining that he "meant nothing by it, it was just an expression."

Rabbi Moshe of Councy, thirteenth-century French author of a code of Jewish law, once said: "It is a minority's fate to be judged by its worst members." With this in mind, I decided the dinner party provided an excellent opportunity to teach a little about my religion to a very receptive audience.

I learned this from an earlier experience where a friend joined a club that had opened its doors to Jewish members only the year before. Along with hers, there were only seven Jewish families. Her first holiday season she noticed that although there was a Christmas tree in the club's living room, there was no menorah. She spoke her feelings to the manager, who assured her that to put one next to the Christmas tree was unprecedented and impossible. My friend wanted to quit the club on principle but was encouraged by the six other families to stay. Stay and continue to be a good person, they advised. If you leave the club, they will win. If you stay, you may teach them eventually to feel affection for Jews and Judaism. It is a far nobler thing to do. Today, several years later, there are seven times the number of original Jewish families at this club. And each December, as you walk through the main entrance, you will see on the member's board notice of an open house and *latke* party in celebration of Hanukkah.

Will anti-Semitism ever be a thing of the past? Perhaps not. But I do not believe that anti-Semitism is the *only* problem Jews face. Not in America. Not in the larger world. If there is a foe, it is not only anti-Semitism but also *acculturation* that has led to a loss of identity and the unique contribution that we as *a people* can make to the society in which we live. With every passing day, more and more Jews are being absorbed into a tolerant and diverse nation, which is good and not so good. On the one hand, across-the-board acceptance of Jews is what many in our religion have dreamed of, but on the other, our greatest challenge today has become an intermarriage rate that tops 50 percent. Think about it: Will we have Jewish grandchildren?

*   *   *

WHAT IS A JEW?

What is a Jew? This question is not at all so odd as it seems. Let us see what kind of peculiar creature the Jew is . . . who has never allowed himself to be led astray by all the earthly possessions which his oppressors and persecutors constantly offered him in order that he should change his faith and forsake his own Jewish religion.

The Jew is that sacred being who has brought down from heaven the everlasting fire, and has illumined with it the entire world. He is the religious source, spring, and fountain out of which all the rest of the peoples have drawn their beliefs and their religions.

The Jew is the pioneer of liberty. Even in those olden days, when the people were divided into but two distinct classes, slaves and masters—even so long ago had the law of Moses prohibited the practice of keeping a person in bondage for more than six years.

The Jew is the emblem of civil and religious toleration. "Love the stranger and the sojourner," Moses commands, "because you have been strangers in the land of Egypt." And this was said in those remote and savage times when the principal ambition of the races and nations consisted in crushing and enslaving one another. As concerns religious toleration, the Jewish faith is not only far from the missionary sprit of converting people of other denominations, but on the contrary the Talmud commands the Rabbis to inform and explain to every one who willingly comes to accept the Jewish religion all the difficulties involved in its acceptance, and to point out to the would-be proselyte that the righteous of all nations have a share in immortality. Of such a lofty and ideal religious toleration not even the moralists of our present day can boast.

The Jew is the emblem of eternity. He whom neither slaughter nor torture of thousands of years could destroy, he whom neither fire nor sword nor inquisition was able to wipe off the face of the earth, he who was the first to produce the oracles of God, he who has been for so long the guardian of prophecy, and who transmitted it to the rest of the world—such a nation cannot be destroyed. The Jew is everlasting as is eternity itself.

LEO TOLSTOY

JEWISH DEMOCRATIC IDEALS

Moses Sexias, sexton of the Hebrew Congregation of Newport, had sent the President a letter of welcome on his visit to the town. This is Washington's reply:

17 August 1790

Dear Sir:

The citizens of the United States of America have a right to applaud themselves for having given to Mankind examples of an enlarged and liberal policy worthy of imitation. All possess alike liberty of conscience and immunities of citizenship. It is now no more that toleration is spoken of, as if it was by the indulgence of one class of people that another enjoyed the exercise of their inherent natural rights. For happily the Government of the United States, which gives bigotry no sanction, to persecution no assistance, requires only that they who live under its protection should demean themselves as good citizens, in giving it on all occasions their effectual support.

... May the Children of the Stock of Abraham, who dwell in this land, continue to merit and enjoy the good will of the other Inhabitants, while every one shall sit in safety under his own vine and fig-tree, and there shall be none to make him afraid. May the father of all mercies scatter light and not darkness in our paths, and make us all in our several vocations useful here, and in his own due time and way everlastingly happy.

GEORGE WASHINGTON

... in spite of Bolingbroke and Voltaire, I will insist that the Hebrews have done more to civilize men than any other nation. If I were an atheist, and believed in blind eternal fate, I should still believe that fate had ordained the Jews to be the most essential instrument for civilizing the nations. If I were an atheist of any other sect, who believe or pretend to believe that all is ordered by chance, I should believe that chance had ordered the Jews to preserve and propagate to all mankind the doctrine of a supreme, intelligent, wise, almighty sovereign of the universe, and consequently all civilization . . .

JOHN ADAMS

I believe in the value of the endeavors to extend and improve religious education among children and youth of the Jewish faith. In teaching this democratic faith to American children, we need the sustaining, buttressing aid of those great ethical religious teachings which are the heritage of our modern civilization. For not upon strength nor upon power alone, but upon the spirit of God shall our democracy be founded.

FRANKLIN D. ROOSEVELT

My pen may have some skill, but I could not begin to measure the debt that this country owes to its Jews and to millions of its foreign born citizens, first for a jealous guarding of American rights and liberties to which the native-born have too often been indifferent; second, for preserving at all times a great reservoir of idealism and liberalism and thirdly, for keeping alive a passionate quest for knowledge in every field, which has steadily quickened American life and notably its colleges.

OSWALD GARRISON VILLARD

More Presidential Reflections

The American people need no reminder of the service which those of Jewish faith have rendered our nation. It has been a service with honor and distinction. History reveals that your people have played a great and commendable part in the defense of Americanism during the World War and prior wars, and have contributed much in time of peace toward the development and preservation of the glory and romance of our country and our democratic form of government.

For devotion in peace, for devotion in war, Jewish citizenship—as I know it—is a shining example to all the world.

FRANKLIN D. ROOSEVELT

I wish your nation [of Jews] may be admitted to all privileges of citizens in every country of the world. This country has done much. I wish it may do more; and annul every narrow idea in religion, government, and commerce. Let the wits joke; the philosophers sneer! What then? It has pleased the Providence of the "first cause," the universal cause, that Abraham should give religion, not only to Hebrews, but to Christians and Mahometans, the greatest part of the modern civilized world.

JOHN ADAMS

Here is a great body of our Jewish citizens from whom have sprung men of genius in every walk of our varied life; men who have conceived of its ideals with singular clearness; and led its enterprises with spirit and sagacity. . . . They are not Jews in America; they are American citizens.

WOODROW WILSON, ADDRESS AT CARNEGIE HALL IN NEW

YORK, DECEMBER, 6, 1911.

What Does Europe Owe to the Jews?

Many things, good and bad, and above all one thing of the nature both of the best and the worst: the grand style in morality, the fearfulness and majesty of infinite demands, of infinite significations, the whole Romanticism and sublimity of moral questionableness—and consequently just the most attractive, ensnaring, and exquisite element in those iridescences and allurements to life, in the after-sheen of which the sky of our European culture, its evening sky, now glows— perhaps glows out. For this, we artists among the spectators and philosophers are grateful to the Jews.

FRIEDRICH NIETZSCHE

Our modern progressive civilization owes its origin mainly to the Greeks and the Jews. The progressiveness is the point to be emphasized . . . the Greeks and the Jews, in the few centuries before and after the beginning of the Christian era, intensified an element of progressive activity which was diffused throughout the many peoples in the broad belt from Mesopotamia to Spain . . . So far as the Greeks and Jews were active, progress was not in a rut degenerating into conservatism . . . The Greeks have vanished, the Jews remain. . . .

ALFRED NORTH WHITEHEAD

A RIGHTEOUS PEOPLE

As long as the world lasts, all who want to make progress in righteousness will come to Israel for inspiration, as the people who have the sense for righteousness most glowing and strongest.

MATTHEW ARNOLD

I have never seen a country or a culture which was not the better for having the contribution of the Jewish people.

PEARL BUCK

9 November 1849:

I feel, and have ever felt, respect and sympathy for all that remains of that extraordinary people who persevered through the darkness and idolatry of so many centuries, the knowledge of one supreme spiritual Being . . . The Hebrew Scriptures I regard as the fountain from which we draw all we know of the world around us, and of our own character and destiny as intelligent, moral, and responsible beings.

DANIEL WEBSTER

The Jews are with us as a perpetual lesson to teach us modesty and civility. We have no claim to take it for granted that we are all right, and they are all wrong. And, therefore, in the midst of all triumphs of Christianity, it is well that the stately synagogue should lift its walls by the side of the aspiring cathedral, a perpetual reminder that there are many mansions in the Father's earthly house as well as in the heavenly one; that civilized humanity, longer in time and broader in space than any historical form of belief, is mightier than any one institution or organization it includes.

OLIVER WENDELL HOLMES

My policy is to govern men as the great majority of them wish to be governed. That, I believe, is the way to recognize the sovereignty of the people. It was as a Catholic that I won the war in the Vendee, as a Moslem that I established myself in Egypt, and as an Ultramontane that I won the confidence of the Italians. If I were governing Jews, I should rebuild the Temple of Solomon. . . .

NAPOLEON BONAPARTE

THE DREAM OF A JEWISH HOMELAND

I am told Zionism is a utopia. I do not know; perhaps. But inasmuch as I see in this utopia an unconquerable thirst for freedom, one for which the people will suffer, it is for me a reality. With all my heart I pray that the Jewish people, like the rest of humanity, may be given spiritual strength to labor for its dream and to establish it in flesh and blood.

MAXIM GORKY

It is manifestly right that the scattered Jews should have a national center and a national home to be re-united, and where else but in Palestine, with which for three thousand years they have been intimately and profoundly associated? We think it will be good for the world, good for the Jews, good for the British Empire, but also good for the Arabs who dwell in Palestine . . . they shall share in the benefits and progress of Zionism.

WINSTON CHURCHILL

The Balfour Declaration

Foreign Office, November 2, 1917

Dear Lord Rothschild,

I have much pleasure in conveying to you, on behalf of His Majesty's Government, the following declaration of sympathy with Jewish Zionist aspirations which has been submitted to, and approved by, the Cabinet.

"His Majesty's Government view with favour the establishment in Palestine of a national home for the Jewish people, and will use their best endeavors to facilitate the achievement of this object, it being clearly understood that nothing shall be done which may prejudice the civil and religious rights of existing non-Jewish communities in Palestine, or the rights and political status enjoyed by Jews in any other country."

ARTHUR JAMES BALFOUR

Battling Discrimination

In 1894, a French soldier betrayed military secrets to Germany. The army accused Captain Alfred Dreyfus of being the spy, simply because he was a Jew. Even though there was evidence strongly pointing to a Colonel Esterhapzy, Dreyfus was sentenced by a military court to life imprisonment on Devil's Island. On learning of this, the novelist Emile Zola, along with a small group of French intellectuals, took up the man's case. Zola initiated a national campaign in Dreyfus's behalf and as part of this campaign, published an article entitled "J'accuse," from which the following is excerpted. Twelve years after his arrest, despite opposition from the French government, army, and Catholic Church, Dreyfus's case was finally reopened. He was exonerated and his rank in the French army restored.

May all my words perish if Dreyfus is not innocent . . . I did not want my country to remain in lies and injustice. One day, France will thank me for having helped to save its honor.

EMILE ZOLA

While I was Police Commissioner [1895] an anti-Semitic preacher from Berlin, Rector Ahlwardt, came over to New York to preach a crusade against the Jews. Many of the New York Jews were much excited and asked me to prevent him from speaking and not to give him police protection. This, I told them, was impossible; and if possible would have been undesirable because it would have made him a martyr. The proper thing to do was to make him ridiculous.

Accordingly I detailed for his protection a Jew sergeant and a score or two of Jew policemen. He made his harangue against the Jews under the active protection of some forty policemen, every one of them a Jew.

It was the most effective possible answer; and incidentally it was an object lesson to our people, whose greatest need is to learn that there must be no division by class hatred, whether this hatred be that of creed against creed, nationality against nationality, section against section, or men of one social or industrial condition against men of another social or industrial condition.

THEODORE ROOSEVELT

Of all the bigotries that savage the human temper there is none so stupid as the anti-Semitic.

. . . In the sight of these fanatics, Jews of today can do nothing right. If they are rich, they are birds of prey. If they are poor, they are vermin. If they are in favor of war, that is because they want to exploit the bloody feuds of Gentiles to their own profit. If they are anxious for peace, they are instinctive cowards or traitors. If they give generously—and there are no more liberal givers than the Jews—they are doing it for some selfish purpose of their own. If they don't give—then what would you expect of a Jew?

If labor is oppressed by great capital, the greed of the Jew is held responsible. If labor revolts against capital as it did in Russia—the Jew is blamed for that also. If he lives in a strange land, he must be persecuted and pogromed out of it. If he wants to go back to his own he must be prevented . . .

The latest exhibition of this wretched indulgence is the agitation against settling poor Jews in the land their fathers made famous.

DAVID LLOYD GEORGE

I think, if we speak of musical impressions, that Jewish folk music has made a most powerful impression on me. I never tire of delighting in it, it's multifaceted, it can appear to be happy while it is tragic. It's almost always laughter through tears.

This quality of Jewish folk music is close to my ideas of what music should be. There should always be two layers in music. Jews were tormented for so long that they learned to hide their despair. They express despair in dance music.

All folk music is lovely, but I can say that Jewish folk music is unique. Many composers listened to it, including Russian composers, Mussorgsky, for instance. He carefully set down Jewish folk songs. Many of my works reflect my impressions of Jewish music.

This is not a purely musical issue, it is also a moral issue. I often test a person by his attitude toward Jews. In our day and age, any person with pretensions of decency cannot be anti-Semitic. This seems so obvious that it doesn't need saying, but I've had to argue the point for at least thirty years.

Once after the war I was passing a bookstore and saw a

volume with Jewish songs. I was always interested in Jewish folklore, and I thought the book would give the melodies, but it contained only the texts. It seemed to me that if I picked out several texts and set them to music, I would be able to tell about the fate of the Jewish people. It seemed an important thing to do, because I could see anti-Semitism growing all around me. But I couldn't have the cycle performed then, it was played for the first time much later, and later still I did an orchestral version of the work.

My parents considered anti-Semitism a shameful superstition, and in that sense I was given a singular upbringing. In my youth I came across anti-Semitism among my peers, who thought that Jews were getting preferential treatment. They didn't remember the pogroms, the ghettos, or the quotas.

But even before the war, the attitude toward Jews had changed drastically. It turned out that we had far to go to achieve brotherhood. The Jews became the most persecuted and defenseless people of Europe. It was a return to the Middle Ages. Jews became a symbol for me. All of man's defenselessness was concentrated in them. After the war, I tried to convey that feeling in my music. . . . That's when I wrote the Violin Concerto, the Jewish Cycle, and the Fourth Quartet.

Not one of these works could be performed then. They were heard only after Stalin's death. I still can't get used to it. The Fourth Symphony was played twenty-five years after I wrote it. There are compositions that have yet to be performed, and no one knows when they will be heard.

. . . [We] must never forget about the dangers of anti-Semitism and keep reminding others of it, because the infection is alive and who knows if it will ever disappear.

That's why I was overjoyed when I read Yevtushenko's *Babi Yar*; the poem astounded me. It astounded thousands of people. Many had heard about *Babi Yar*, but it took Yevtushenko's poem to make them aware of it. They tried to destroy the memory of *Babi Yar*, first the Germans and then the Ukrainian government. But after Yevtushenko's poem, it became clear that it would never be forgotten. That's the power of art.

People knew about *Babi Yar* before Yevtushenko's poem, but they were silent. And when they read the poem, the silence was broken. Art destroys silence. . . .

DMITRY SHOSTAKOVICH

When people say "Jews," I ask, "*Which* Jew?" Similarly, I hope that when people say "blacks," someone asks, "*Which* black?"

ARTHUR ASHE

Among blacks in Richmond [Virginia], as among people elsewhere, certain anti-Jewish phrases were current, although in a mild way for the most part. For example, to "*Jew* you down" meant to get the better of you in a deal. Almost certainly the speaker was no anti-Semite but rather an unthinking person using expressions he or she had picked up somewhere. My father saw clearly that even great wealth did not save the Jews of Richmond from bigotry. He liked to tell the story of driving William Thalhimer to see a man about a piece of land that Thalhimer wanted to buy. The man hated to sell the land to anyone, but he hated above all selling it to a Jew. As Daddy listened, the man insulted Thalhimer in every way he could. Thalhimer said nothing. The deal was concluded. Driving back, my father asked Thalhimer why he had meekly taken those insults from an inferior.

"Arthur," Thalhimer said, "I came out here to purchase that piece of land. I got the piece of land. It belongs to me now, not to him. That man can go on cursing me as long as he likes. I have the land."

ARTHUR ASHE

"THE JEWISH CEMETERY AT NEWPORT"

How strange it seems! These Hebrews in their graves,
Close by the street of this fair seaport town,
Silent beside the never-silent waves,
At rest in all this moving up and down!

How came they here? What burst of Christian hate,
What persecution, merciless and blind,
Drove o'er the sea—that desert desolate—
These Ishmaels and hagars of mankind?

Pride and humiliation hand in hand
Walked with them through the world where'er they went;
Trampled and beaten were they as the sand,
And yet unshaken as the continent.

For in the background figures vague and sublime,
And all the great traditions of the Past
They saw reflected in the coming time.

And thus forever with reverted look
The mystic volume of the world they read,
Spelling it backward, like a Hebrew book,
Till life became a Legend of the Dead.

But ah! What once has been shall be no more!
The groaning earth in travail and in pain
Brings forth its races, but does not restore,
And the dead nations never rise again.

HENRY WADSWORTH LONGFELLOW

GROWING UP CHRISTIAN IN A JEWISH WORLD

If anyone had told me that I was growing up in a ghetto, I would not have known what they meant. When I came home from my first day at Summer School, my mother asked me about the children in my class. I said there were "five Sullivans." She was skeptical. So was my father. There were, in fact, five Solomons in my class. I knew no more of Jews than did my aunt Mary, growing up thirty years before in the Welsh community of the Western Avenue M.E. Church. She had a handsome young suitor, of whom she was very fond. One day a friend asked her, a bit hesitantly, if she knew that the young man was Jewish. "What do you mean?" my aunt asked. "Is that some kind of disease?"

In Miss MacPherson's first-grade classroom there were probably twenty-four children, of whom I suppose twenty were Jewish, one was black—a handsome boy named Booker T. Washington, who later became a professional singer—two were blond Scandinavian girls and one was myself. I do not believe any of us felt differences of creed, color or national origin. We wouldn't have understood that. Summer School was about 95 percent Jewish, but years later, former classmates told me that neither they nor their parents had thought of it as a "Jewish" school. Nor did I. No one noticed that there were no Jewish teachers until in 1918, Miss Levy appeared and took over grade three.

We all enjoyed the usual holidays—Christmas vacation, Lincoln's and Washington's birthdays, Easter vacation and, later on, Armistice Day, November 11. But the Jewish children got extra holidays—Rosh Hashanah, Yom Kippur and Passover. On those days, our little band of four or five goyim huddled in the deserted classroom while our teacher tried to find a way to occupy us. Outside on Sixth Avenue, my friends walked with their parents in their best clothes, or played shinny and marbles. It wasn't fair. When I grew a bit older, three of us would be selected as "writers" and go to the big

Keneseth Israel Temple, very Orthodox, escorted by serious men in black suits. There we would record the financial pledges, the names, addresses and amounts. Writing was forbidden on the high holy days. For this we got a dollar. Almost every holiday, a worried old grandmother—a *babushka*, as I would come to say in Russia—would encounter me as I was walking home from school, grasp my wrist and ask me to light the stove in her kitchen. It was forbidden to light a fire until sundown, but if the little goy would do it she could get supper going. For this I got a nickel.

The nickels and dollars did not wash away the discrimination. I was a member of a small minority amid a large and powerful majority. We were friends, but there were lines I could not cross. School ended at three o'clock. I came home, had a glass of milk and a butter-and-sugar sandwich, and was ready to play. But my friends who went to *heder*, the Hebrew school, weren't free until five. I could see no reason, nor did they, why I shouldn't go to *heder* too. Finally, my mother went to the school and asked if I could be admitted. The rabbi was outraged. Positively not. This was not a school for the goyim.

In time I came to know a great deal about discrimination, about anti-Semitism in American country clubs and in the higher ranks of the Soviet government, about numerous clauses at Harvard and in the Academy of Science in Moscow. One of my childhood friends adopted a new, "non-Jewish" name and several of my Russian friends conveniently "lost" their internal passports and got new ones which specified their nationality as Russian, not Jewish. I had walked across the neatly kept ghetto in Warsaw, its carefully piled bricks and fresh-swept rubble marking where the streets and houses had been. I had met survivors of Auschwitz. I knew the results of the dirty little game that starts with "some of my best friends are Jews" and ends with extermination ovens. I went south in 1960 for the opening of the great struggle to bring America to live under the reality of our Constitution. I knew Malcolm X before he was murdered. I learned a good bit about the rawest edges of racism.

HARRISON SALISBURY

THE FUTURE OF FRIENDSHIP

A LETTER FROM THE CARDINAL, SEPTEMBER 8, 1999.

My Dearest Friends:

The Jewish High Holy Days come once again, reminding our world of who created it, who blesses it with life and who judges it in his merciful justice. God who gives all humanity the dignity of being made in his image, has chosen Israel as his particular people that they may be an example of faithfulness for all the nations of the earth. With sincere love and true admiration for your fidelity to the Covenant, I am happy once again to send my greetings for a blessed new year.

This Sabbath evening, as the celebration of Rosh Hashanah commences, a new decade will begin. During the year of 5760 we Christians will start a new era of the year 2000, the turn of another millennium in our history. Our Holy Father, Pope John Paul II, has asked all Christians to enter this new millennium in the spirit of Jubilee. Part of the process is a call for teshuva, or repentance. Ash Wednesday, March 8, has been specially set aside as a day for Catholics to reflect upon the pain inflicted on the Jewish people by many of our members over the last millennium. We most sincerely want to start a new era.

I pray that as you begin a new decade, and as we begin another millennium in our Jewish-Christian relationship, we will refresh our encounter with a new respect and even love for one another as children of God. Working in our own ways, but also working together, let us both remain committed to the fulfillment of God's reign. I ask this Yom Kippur that you understand my own abject sorrow for any member of the Catholic

Church, high or low, including myself, who may have harmed
you or your forebears in any way.

 Be assured of my prayers and friendship. L'shanah tove ti-
kotevu!

Faithfully,

John Cardinal O'Connor

Archbishop of New York

THIS LETTER WAS REPRINTED IN FULL IN THE *NEW YORK TIMES*

SEPTEMBER 19, 1999.

SEVEN

Paths of Prayer

All are equal before God in prayer.

SHEMOT RABBAH, 21.4

IN THE BROADWAY MUSICAL *FIDDLER ON THE ROOF,* Tevye asks his rabbi whether there is a blessing for the czar. "Why not?" the rabbi answers. "We Jews have a blessing for everything."

Perhaps not. But we get the point. Judaism has blessings for an astonishing number of occasions: before and after eating, seeing a scholar, a rainbow, commencing or concluding a journey, waking up in the morning and going to sleep at night. And, of course, there are blessings attendant to such ritual acts as lighting Shabbat candles, reading from the Torah, eating matzoth and nailing a *mezuzah* to a doorpost.

Prayer has been a vital part of Judaism since Abraham entered into a covenantal relationship with God. From that time, it has been in a constant state of change, yielding to both individual and communal needs in a given period. What is prayer, and why does one pray?

Prayer was written by humans to satisfy their needs as well as the perceived desires of God. Once, a young Jew, observant of Jewish law, experienced an unrequited love for the woman of his dreams, whom he had wanted so much to marry. He asked an older, learned friend if there was no reward for observing God's commandments. His friend reminded him of the prayer for the new month. In that prayer we pray that the new month may be for our *good.* "Why would one have to pray for a good month? Would anyone pray for a *bad* month?" the young man asked. The answer is that we don't know what is for our ultimate good. What we may pray for today may not be good for our tomorrow. The older friend answered, "Only God knows what is good for our future. Trust God. Maybe this relationship, as much as you love this young woman, is not *l'tovah* . . . for your good."

Here is the same story updated: Only a year ago, I asked my rabbi how I could be expected to continue to pray to God when, even after praying for months, my prayer was not answered. Why, I asked again, did God not answer my prayers?

"Oh, but he did," my rabbi assured me. "The answer was *no*."

Our tradition teaches that when a small group of Jews comes together for prayer, the *Shekhinah* (or presence of God) dwells among them. The communal aspect of worship is best articulated by the concept of the *minyan*, the traditional requirement that ten Jewish male adults be present for daily, Shabbat, and holiday services. (Reform Judaism and some conservative synagogues count women in the *minyan*.)

Jews know that the presence of God cannot be limited to a particular space but resides in the human heart and is manifested by human conduct. In other words, prayer can take place anywhere. Still, most feel closest to God among a congregation, in a synagogue. Tradition assigns three names to the synagogue that describe its functions: *Bet Ha-T'fillah*, *Bet Ha-Midrash*, and *Bet Ha-Knesset* (House of Prayer, Study, and Assembly). *Bet Ha-T'fillah* is derived from God's command to Moses, "They shall build a Sanctuary, that I may dwell among them." It is interesting to note that the verse is not, "that I may dwell therein," but rather "among them." (Exodus 25:8). A Yiddish saying best expresses the importance of the synagogue in Jewish life: "If only two Jews remained in the world, one would summon to the synagogue, and the other would go there."

Personally, I love the whole ritual of prayer. I love it because it connects me to the past and makes me revere the present. As I stand in synagogue, reciting the *Shema*, I can't help but consider how many people have recited it before me, people in bigger and smaller synagogues in London, Paris, and Rome, in Jerusalem and Tel Aviv, in *shtetls* and in ghettos and on cruise ships. I love the community of prayer, and the repetition, singing every Friday night the same songs, chanting the same words, challenging myself to memorize more and more of the Hebrew.

As I recite these prayers, I sometimes see the little girl I once was, in the sanctuary of Temple Israel in Miami on the high holy days, sitting next to my mother, trying on her bracelets, examining the animal heads on her fur stole, wrapping the red satin ribbon from the prayer book tighter and tighter around my finger until its tip turned white from lack of blood. And I remember standing near the aisle and touching the Torah with my prayer book as it passed by in the arms of the rabbi. (I think it was not the ritual of the act that I liked so much as that it provided me an opportunity to get out of my seat.)

I now go to shul every Friday night that I can. And I'm surprised at how many of the prayers I recite from memory of my childhood. Last week I mastered the Kaddish in Hebrew. Even though the time for mourning my parents has long been over, and even though they themselves were hardly religious people, I feel they would be pleased that I know it.

*   *   *

THE SYNAGOGUE

The synagogue is the regenerative soil of Jewish life.
Just beneath its statuesque surface,
Our roots densely intertwine.
Like giant redwoods,
Standing shoulder to shoulder in ever shrinking forests,
We Jews share the reality of interdependence,
Holding one another up.

Nowhere is this reality more strikingly revealed
Than in our congregations, our houses of gathering.
Bialik called the synagogue "the mystic fount . . .
the treasure of our soul."
The Talmud called it the place
"where heaven and earth kiss,"
The Zohar: "an earthly copy of the heavenly original."
I simply call it home.

ALEXANDER M. SCHINDLER

In this sanctuary, the generations that have come before us
pray alongside the generations that are yet to come. Slaves
and prophets are an unseen presence; scholars, physicians and
peasants, factory workers, merchants, mystics, the persecuted
and the redeemed: all are here, all are with us.

ARTHUR LELYVELD

The synagogue is the sanctuary of Israel. Born out of our longing for the living God, it has been to Israel, throughout our wanderings, a visible token of the presence of God in His people's midst. Its beauty is the beauty of holiness; steadfast it has stood as the champion of justice, mercy, and peace.

Its truths are true for all people. Its love is a love for all people. Its God is the God of all people, as it has been said: "My house shall be called a house of prayer for all peoples."

Let all the family of Israel, all who hunger for righteousness, all who seek the Eternal find Him here—and here find life!

ADAPTED FROM A PRAYER BY LOUIS WITT,

GATES OF PRAYER FOR WEEKDAYS

The heart of the Jewish People has always been in the *Bet Ha-Midrash*, there was the source from which they drew the strength and the inspiration that enabled them to overcome all difficulties and withstand all persecutions. If we want to go on living, we must restore the center to the *Bet Ha-Midrash*, and make that once more the living source of Judaism.

AHAD HA-AM

A synagogue retains its holiness even after it has been desolated.

TALMUD

BLESSINGS OF TORAH

What is Torah? A word that opens worlds, a scroll completed only to be resumed, a learning that has no end. May its words give us strength, its Mitzvot lift us to the heights of noble actions. We thank you, O God, for the gift of Torah, the gift of life.

JOHN RAYNER

The Torah was given in public, for all to see, in the open. For if it had been given in the land of Israel, Israel would have said to the nations of the world, You have no share in it; therefore the Torah was given in the wilderness, in public for all to see, in the open. And everyone who wishes to receive it, let him come and receive it.

TALMUD

Torah is the heritage of Israel. It tells our people's tale. It speaks of the living God, whose seal is truth, whose love is for the good. What is Torah? A pilgrimage without end, a flame that burns within the Jewish heart, a light to illumine the paths of our life. Torah is a promise of wisdom, a journey to understanding, a call to seek truth, a striving for goodness.

NEW LIGHT SIDDUR

It happened that a certain heathen came before Shammai [he and Hillel were the two leading rabbis of their age] and said to him, "I will let you convert me to Judaism on the condition that you teach me the whole Torah while I stand on one foot." Shammai chased him away with the builder's rod in his hand.

When he came before Hillel, he presented the same offer. In reply Hillel said, "What is hateful to you, do not do to your neighbor: this is the whole Torah. The rest is commentary; now go and study."

BABYLONIAN TALMUD, *SHABBAT* 31A

The difference between our Torah and other ancient and modern law codes is that the chief aim of those law codes is to establish law and order in society, whereas the chief aim of the Torah is to enable man to become fully human.

MORDECAI M. KAPLAN

The Hasidim . . . have a saying: *Toireh iz de besteh sroire*— Torah is the best merchandise. They say this not only when comparing the spiritual pursuit of studying Torah to more mundane mercantile activities, but also when dealing with the question of Jewish continuity, much on the minds of American Jews today. What they are saying is simple: Study Torah, follow its precepts, and continuity will take care of itself. Abandon Torah, and all the Federation committees, all the *Hadassahs*, all the United Jewish Appeals and *B'nai Briths*, will not be able to staunch the hemorrhage.

ROBERT EISENBERG

COMMUNICATION WITH GOD

Prayer is an invitation to God to intervene in our lives, to let his will prevail in our affairs; it is the opening of a window to him in our will, our effort to make him the Lord of our soul . . .

In crisis, in moments of despair, a word of prayer is like a strap we take hold of when tottering in a rushing street car which seems to be turning over.

ABRAHAM J. HESCHEL

To repeat, the issue of prayer is not prayer; the issue of prayer is God.

ABRAHAM J. HESCHEL

The Greek word for prayer means "to wish for." The German word for prayer means "to beg." The English word means "to entreat, implore, ask earnestly or supplicate." The Hebrew word is *t'phila*. Its root is *pallal* which means "to judge." The act of praying in Hebrew is *hitpallel*, the reflexive form of the verb; it means "to judge oneself." It signifies self-examination, an inquiry into the state of one's soul, to make it ready for communication with God.

ALBERT S. GOLDSTEIN

The purpose of prayer is to allow us to be alone with God and apart from other men, to give us seclusion in the midst of the world. We are to seek loneliness also in the house of God even when it is crowded with men, to be alone there also with ourselves and our God. If our life is to be filled with devoutness, we must from time to time abandon the ways of the world so that we may enjoy the peace of God.

LEO BAECK

RULES OF PRAYER

Prayer without devotion is no prayer at all. He who has prayed without devotion ought to pray once more. He whose thoughts are wandering or occupied with other matters should not pray before he has collected his thoughts. If he has returned from a journey tired or troubled let him pray only after he has collected his thoughts.

MOSES MAIMONEDES, *MISHNEH TORAH*

Traditionally, Jews face in the direction of Jerusalem when praying. This is why, in synagogues, the Torah Ark is built along the eastern wall.

JOSEPH H. HERTZ

A Jew outside the land of Israel wishing to pray turns his heart towards the land of Israel; when he is in the Land, he turns his heart towards Jerusalem; when he is in Jerusalem, he turns his heart towards the Holy of Holies; if he is in the Holy of Holies, he turns his heart to the cover of the Ark. Thus all Jews praying are directing their hearts towards one place.

BABYLONIAN TALMUD BERACHOT, 30A

A man should not stand on a table or a sofa or a chair while praying, for there may be no elevation before the Lord. But if he is old or sick, a man may pray in whatever position he can.

TALMUD, TOSEFTA BERAKOT, 3

In proper devotion a man has his eyes downward and his heart upward.

TALMUD, YEVAMOT 105B

Nine rabbis can't make a *minyan*, but ten cobblers can.

YIDDISH FOLK-SAYING

He who prays with the community will have his prayer granted.

BABYLONIAN TALMUD, BERAKOT, 8A

Almost no prayers in the Jewish prayer book are recited in the first person; they almost always are offered in the plural. For if people prayed in the first person, their prayers might well be directed either against others or, alternatively, against others' interests. Thus, when a person prays that he receive a job for which he has applied, in effect, he also is praying that the other applicants be rejected. Only when people address God in the plural are they likely to pray for that which is universally beneficial.

JOSEPH TELUSHKIN

THE POWER OF PRAYER

A man should praise God even for misfortunes as much as he praises Him for happiness (say the rabbis in the Talmud). Whether this lofty courage is attainable by the average Jew or not, he learns to feel and to express, or perhaps to express and thus to feel, a constant sense of gratitude to the master of the Universe.

SOLOMON FREEHOF

Pray and pray again. There will come an hour when your request will be granted.

TALMUD, DEBARIM RABBAH, 2:12

THE SHORTEST PRAYER IN THE BIBLE

Please God, make her well.

NUMBERS 12:13

Above is Moses' five-word (el na, refah na lah) plea to God to heal his sister, Miriam, who had been stricken with sudden leprosy, apparently for speaking against him. God heeds Moses' prayer, so that Miriam is subsequently healed.

THE SIDDUR—JEWISH PRAYER BOOK

I regard the old Jewish Siddur as the most important single Jewish book—a more personal expression, a closer record, of

Jewish sufferings, Jewish needs, Jewish hopes and aspirations, than the Bible itself. . . . And if you want to know what Judaism is—the question which has no answer if debated on the plane of intellectual argument—you can find it by absorbing that book. The Jewish soul is mirrored here as nowhere else, mirrored or rather embodied there: the individual's soul in his private sorrows, and the people's soul in its historic burdens, its heroic passion and suffering, its unfaltering faith, throughout the ages.

HENRY SLONIMSKY

From the Siddur

The Shema

Shema Y'lsrael, Adonai eloheinu, Adonai ehad.
Hear O Israel: The Lord our God, the Lord is one.

DEUTERONOMY 6:4

And you shall love the Lord your God with all your heart, with all your soul, and with all your might. And these words which I command you this day shall be upon your heart. And you shall teach them diligently unto your children, and shall talk of them when you sit in your house, and when you walk by the way, and when you lie down, and when you rise up. And you shall bind them for a sign upon your hand, and they shall be for frontlets between your eyes. And you shall write them upon the doorposts of your House and upon your gates.

DEUTERONOMY 6:4–9

The Shema is not a prayer in the ordinary sense of the word, but for thousands of years it has been an integral part of the prayer service. The Shema is a declaration of faith, a pledge of allegiance to One God, an affirmation of Judaism. It is the first prayer that children are taught to say. It is the last utterance of martyrs. It is said on arising in the morning and on going to sleep at night. It is said when one is praising God and when one is beseeching Him. . . . The Shema is said when our lives are full of hope; it is said when all hope is gone and the end is near. Whether in moments of joy or despair, in thankfulness or in resignation, it is the expression of Jewish conviction, the historic proclamation of Judaism's central creed.

HAYIM HALEVY DONIN

The Shema has been the watchword and the rallying-cry of a hundred generations in Israel. By it were they welded into one Brotherhood to do the will of their God who is in heaven. The reading of the Shema has—in rabbinic phrase—clothed Israel with invincible lion-strength, and endowed him with the double-edged sword of the spirit against the unutterable terrors of his long night of exile.

JOSEPH H. HERTZ

The school of Shammai said: "When reading the evening Shema, one should incline (or lean) as if lying down in bed. When reading it in the morning, one should stand up as if rising from bed, as it is written: "and shalt talk of them [the Shema verses] . . . when you liest down and when you risest up."

MISHNA BERAKOT

Adon Olom — Eternal Lord

This prayer is part of the morning service and is often chanted at the conclusion of Sabbath and Festival services as well.

You are the eternal Lord who reigned before any being was created.

At the time when all was made by Your will, You were at once acknowledged Sovereign.

And at the end, when all shall cease to be, You alone shall still be Sovereign.

You were, You are, and You shall be in glorious eternity.

You are One, and there is no other who can compare with you or be equal to you.

You are without beginning, without end; power and dominion belong to you.

You are *my* God, my living Redeemer, my stronghold in times of distress.

You are my banner and my refuge, my benefactor when I call on You.

To You I entrust my spirit when I sleep and when I wake.

As long as my soul is with my body, You are with me, I am not afraid.

UNKNOWN AUTHOR, ELEVENTH OR TWELFTH CENTURY

The Adoration (ALENU)

Let us adore the ever-living God, and render praise unto You who spread out the heavens and established the earth, whose glory is revealed in the heavens above and whose greatness is manifest throughout the world.

You are our God; there is none else.

We bow the head in reverence and worship the Sovereign of Sovereigns, the Holy One, praised be You.

NEW UNION PRAYER BOOK

The Kaddish

Let the glory of God be extolled, and God's great name be hallowed in the world whose creation God willed. May God

rule in our own day, in our own lives, and in the life of all
Israel, and let us say: Amen.

Let God's great name be blessed for ever and ever.

Beyond all the praises, songs and adorations that we can
utter is the Holy One, the Blessed One, whom yet we glorify,
honor and exalt. And let us say: Amen.

For us and for all Israel, may the blessing of peace and the
promise of life come true, and let us say: Amen.

May the One who causes peace to reign in the high heavens, let peace descend on us, and on all Israel, and all the
world and let us say: Amen.

GATES OF PRAYER FOR SHABBAT AND WEEKDAYS,
TRANSLATION OF THE KADDISH

Kaddish, the most sacred prayer in the Jewish liturgy, is said
at every service. Traditionally, Kaddish is recited daily for
eleven months after the death of a parent and each year on
the anniversary day of their deaths. This prayer contains no
reference to the dead but focuses instead on the greatness of
God, of redemption from exile and of everlasting peace in
Messianic times.

SHONIE B. LEVI AND SYLVIA R. KAPLAN

Its origin is mysterious; angels are said to have brought it down
from heaven and taught it to men. About this prayer the tender-
est threads of filial feeling and human recollection are entwined;
for it is the prayer of the orphans! When the father or mother
dies, the surviving sons are to recite it twice daily, morning and
evening, throughout the year of mourning, and then also on each
recurring anniversary of the death—on the *Yahrzeit*.

LEOPOLD KOMPERT

SABBATH PRAYERS

The sun on the treetops no longer is seen,
Come gather to welcome the Sabbath, our queen.
Behold her descending, the holy, the blessed,
And with her the angels of peace and of rest.
Draw near, draw near, and here abide,
Draw near, draw near, O Sabbath bride.
Peace also to you, you angels of peace.

BIALIK, NEW UNION PRAYERBOOK

We come together aboard ship this Shabbat evening to offer thanks to God for the creation of all things.

The sea, the land, the universe all declare God's glory. We marvel at the beauty of nature and praise God for all His precious gifts that have been granted unto us.

May we, together with all humankind, strive to achieve the spirit of brotherhood in a world at peace.

SABBATH EVENING SERVICE AT SEA, ABOARD THE *CRYSTAL*
HARMONY AUGUST 1998

PRAYERS FOR PEACE

Grant us peace, Your most precious gift, O eternal source of peace, and enable Israel to be its messenger unto the peoples of the earth. Bless our country that it may ever be a stronghold of peace, and its advocate in the council of nations. May contentment reign within its borders, health and happiness within its homes. Strengthen the bonds of friendship and fellowship among all the inhabitants of our land. Plant virtue in every soul, and may the love of Your name hallow every home and every heart Blessed is the Eternal God, the Source of peace.

NEW UNION PRAYERBOOK

Grant peace to all the nations.
Let Your children thirst for justice,
And hunger for righteousness;
With wisdom and insight,
Mercy and love,
Let them walk the gates of peace,
O God,
Whose will is peace,
Whose way is peace.

NEW LIGHT SIDDUR

Help us, our God, to lie down in peace, and awaken us to life again, our Sovereign. Spread over us Your shelter of peace, guide us with Your good counsel . . . Shelter us in the shadow of Your wings, O God, who watches over us and delivers us, our gracious and merciful Ruler. Guard our coming and our going; grant us life and peace, now and always. Spread over us the shelter of Your peace. Praised are you, Adonai, eternal Guardian of Your people Israel.

SIDDUR SHIM SHALOM

MUSIC AND PRAYER

Praise God with the call of the Shofar; praise God with the harp and lyre. Praise God with the timbrel and dance; praise God with stringed instruments and flute. Praise God with resounding cymbals; praise God with clanging cymbals.

PSALM 150

"The inseparable bond between God and the art of music is expressed time and again in the whole vast post-biblical literature . . . The gates of song preceded the gates of repentance," said saintly Rabbi Pinchos Koretzer. The Temple of song is the nearest to the source of holiness, said Rabbi Nachman of Bratslav, another sage. There are gates in heaven, which can be opened by song alone, is a kabbalistic saying. Indeed, the Jewish conception of the relationship between divinity and music is as old as Israel. No wonder that a people cherishing such a conception was destined to occupy a distinguished place in the world of this divine art of music."

JACOB BEIMEL

Praise God

God does not want to be believed in, to be debated and defended by us, but simply to be realized through us.

GATES OF FORGIVENESS

Kinship with God is derived from the actual experience of prayer and from the effort after righteousness. We have no power to explain God. If we could, we should be God ourselves.

LILY H. MONTAGUE

Praise God from the heavens; praise God in the heights. Praise God, all His angels; praise God, all his legions. Praise God, sun and moon; praise God, all bright stars. Praise God, the most exalted of the heavens and the waters that are above the heavens. Let them praise the name of God, for God commanded and they were created. And God established them forever and ever, God issued a decree that will not change. Praise God from the earth, sea giants and all watery

depths . . . Mountains and hills, fruitful trees and all cedars . . .
Let them praise the name of God.

ART SCROLL

THE FRUIT OF RELIGION

Religion, they say, is only custom. I might agree with this if
the "only" were left out. Customs are the flowers of civilization. You can tell a man's education, even much of his character, by his habits. Morality, ethics, are words derived from
roots denoting that which is acknowledged and adopted by
the people as right and proper.

Religion will not come to our aid the moment we call for
her; she must be loved and cherished at all times if she is to
prove our true friend in need. Much of the present indifference of our young people is directly traceable to the absence
of all religious observances in their homes. Piety is the fruit
of religious customs.

GUSTAV GOTTHEIL

EIGHT

WORDS OF WISDOM

Hillel said:

If I am not for myself, who will be for me?
And being for myself only, what am I?
And if not now, when?

ETHICS OF THE FATHERS

Hillel also said:

Whatever is hateful unto thee, do it not unto your fellow man.
This is the whole Law; the rest is commentary.

TALMUD

THE FINAL SECTION OF THIS BOOK is a journey into Jewish law and lore that will explain much about the contemporary Jewish value stance. Actually, every book in the vast collection of classical Jewish literature can be rightfully subtitled: *wisdom literature*. That "library" grew like a snowball rolling downhill, gathering texture as it traveled from its biblical origin to the present. Every category, every volume, deals virtually with the totality of life. The library's shelves contain the biblical laws of Moses, the moral declarations of the biblical Prophets, the Mishnaic discourses of Hillel the Elder, and of Shammai, his legal adversary.

There is something to be learned from each of these tomes which, along with many others, could legitimately be filed under the categories of political, historical, ethical, and moral guides to living. Maimonides' twelfth-century legal code, the *Mishne Torah*, tells us much about the proper path in life that one should follow. Tales of Israel Ba'al Shem Tov, the founder of hasidism, and of the Hasidic masters teach us as much about the condition of the poor Jew in the *shtetls* of Russia as they do about the eighteenth-century rabbinic leader of Lithuania, the Vilna Gaon. The Mishnaic work, "Pirke Avot . . . The Sayings of the Sages" informs us that one who does not increase his knowledge, decreases it. Accordingly, one of the first institutions a new Jewish community deemed necessary was a school.

The Jewish obsession for the acquisition of knowledge is not a new phenomenon. Two millennia ago, it was expressed by a text that taught that one ignorant of the Law could not be righteous. Study, the pursuit of knowledge, was not a momentary whim but a *mitzvah*, a commandment, incumbent upon every Jew.

You may wonder why, given such a sea of information, I selected the particular passages I include here. I wish I could present a valid argument as to why one selection as opposed to another; one maxim and not the next. I cannot. I simply liked those I selected and include them here in the hopes that the passages which have meaning to me will have meaning to you as well.

It was an interesting exercise, I must admit. I looked for universality in all. In selecting eighteen Yiddish maxims from the hundreds I read, I felt like a kid in a candy shop—so much to choose from, so little space to put it all. Some sayings I remembered hearing throughout my life and was surprised, in fact, to see how many were Yiddish in origin. The most universal, of course, is the golden rule. Who among us did not recite these words in elementary school? But it was not until many years later that I realized the basis for that homily came from the teachings of Hillel, and were considered the bywords of Judaism itself: "That which is hateful to you, do it not to any man."

*　　*　　*

LIFE LESSONS

A man should so live that at the close of every day he can repeat: "I have not wasted my day."

ZOHAR

When asked how things are, don't whine and grumble about your hardships. If you answer, "Lousy," then God says, "You call this bad? I'll show you what bad really is!"

When asked how things are and, despite hardship or suffering, if you answer, "Good," then God says, "You call this good? I'll show you what good *really* is!"

REBBE NACHMAN OF BRESLOV

Just as the hand held before the eye can hide the tallest mountain, so the routine of everyday life can keep us from seeing the vast radiance and the secret wonders that fill the world.

HASIDIC SAYING

Nine-tenths of the serious controversies which arise in life result from misunderstanding.

LOUIS D. BRANDEIS

Help and respect can come to a people only through self-help
and self-respect.

STEPHEN S. WISE

Fear God by day, and you'll sleep soundly at night.

JOSEPH ZABARA, SEFER SHAASHUIM

The greatest menace to freedom is an inert people.

LOUIS D. BRANDEIS

When a righteous man dies, he dies only for his own generation. It is like a man who loses a pearl. Wherever it may be,
the pearl continues to be a pearl. It is lost only to its owner.

ELEAZAR, TALMUD, MEGILLA 15A

TEACHINGS AND PRINCIPLES

EIGHTEEN YIDDISH MAXIMS

A man should be master of his will and slave of his conscience.

The most humble man thinks himself greater than his best
friend thinks he is.

While pursuing happiness, we flee from contentment.

For the unlearned, old age is winter; for the learned, it is the
season of harvest.

Fear only two: God, and the man who has no fear of God.

Fear the one who fears you.

False friends are like migratory birds: They fly away in cold weather.

One who believes that anything can be accomplished by money is likely to do anything for money.

It is easier to abandon evil traits today than tomorrow.

One father supports ten children, but ten children do not support one father.

He who saves is worth more than he who earns.

He who is sated does not believe the hungry.

Half a truth is a whole lie.

Better a bad peace than a good war.

When a father gives to his son, both laugh; when a son gives to his father, both cry.

A man is what he is, not what he used to be.

Every man knows that he must die, but no one believes it.

Better a noble death than a wretched life.

Ten Paths to Right Conduct: The Talmud
according to *Rosh*

Rabbi Asher ben Yehiel (known as Rosh from the initials of his Hebrew title Rabbenu Asher) was born in 1250 and died in 1327. He migrated from Germany to Spain. His fame rests on his compendium of the Talmudic laws, which omits the discussion and concisely states the final decisions. His work became so popular that it has been printed with almost every edition of the Talmud under the title Rosh.

Never be quick to quarrel.

Do not hurt people either by causing them to lose money or by saying unkind words to them; do not envy or hate them.

Weight your words on the scale of your intelligence before you speak.

Conceal in your heart whatever is said in your presence, even when you are not pledged to secrecy.

Do not cast envious eyes on one who has become richer than you; instead, consider the one who has less than you.

Never do in private what you would be ashamed to do in public.

Do not raise a threatening hand against your neighbor.

Do not circulate false reports; do not slander anyone.

Never make an insolent reply to one who has said unpleasant things to you.

Do not shout in the street, but speak softly.

Do not expose your fellow man to shame in public.

Never weary of making friends; consider a single enemy as one too many.

If you have a faithful friend, do not lose him; he is a precious possession.

You must not fool your friend by false flattery, or by speaking with an insincere heart.

Never stay angry with your friend for a single day, but humble yourself and ask his forgiveness.

Do not say: "I am the injured party, let him come and apologize to me."

ASHER BEN YAHIEL

THREE VOICES

Three Voices gladden the heart: the voice of the Torah, the voice of rain, and the voice of coins.

MIDRASH

There are three partners in man: God, his father and his mother.

TALMUD

613 COMMANDMENTS INTO 11 ETHICAL PRINCIPLES

Rabbi Simlai taught: 613 commandments were revealed to Moses; 365 negative commandments . . . and 248 positive commandments . . . When David came, he summed up the 613 commandments in eleven [ethical] principles:

"Lord, who may sojourn in Your tent, who may dwell on Your holy mountain?"

(1) He who lives without blame

(2) who does righteous acts

(3) who speaks the truth in his heart

(4) whose tongue speaks no deceit

(5) who has not done harm to his fellow

(6) or borne reproach for [his acts toward] his neighbor

(7) for whom a contemptible person is abhorrent

(8) who honors those who fear the Lord

(9) who stands by his oath even when it is to his disadvantage

(10) who has never lent money for interest

(11) or accepted a bribe against the innocent."

PSALMS 15:1–5p

TEACHINGS OF THE SAGES (*PIRKEI AVOT*)

Shimon ha-Tzaddik was one of the last members of the Great Assembly. This was a favorite teaching of his: The world rests on three things—on Torah, on service of God, on deeds of love.

Antigonus, of Sokho, received the tradition from Shimon Ha-Tzaddik. This was a favorite teaching of his: Do not be like servants who serve their master expecting to receive a reward; be rather like servants who serve their master unconditionally, with no thought of reward.

Rabbi Hananiah, the Deputy High priest, taught: Pray for the welfare of the Government, for if people did not fear it, they would swallow each other alive.

Rabbi Yose taught: The property of others should be as precious to you as your own. Perfect yourself in the study of Torah—it will not come to you by inheritance; let all your deeds be for Heaven's sake.

SIDDUR SIM SHALOM

Ethics of the Fathers

The Mishnah *was compiled and edited by Rabbi Judah Hanasi and his colleagues at the beginning of the third century. It consists of sixty-three books called tractates, each of which is divided into chapters and subdivided into paragraphs. The tractate* Avoth *("Fathers") deals with the ethical principles given by the fathers of Jewish tradition, who flourished over a period of five centuries, from the time of the last prophet to the end of the second century.*

The world is based on three principles: Torah, worship and kindliness.

Let your house be a meeting-place for the wise; sit at their feet; and drink in their words thirstily.

Let your house be wide open; treat the poor as members of your own family; and do not engage in gossip with women.

Provide yourself with a teacher; get yourself a colleague; and judge all men favorably.

Stay away from a bad neighbor; do not associate with an evil man; and do not despair when you meet with disaster.

He who does not increase his knowledge decreases it.

Make study a regular habit; say little and do much; and receive all men cheerfully.

The bashful cannot learn, nor can the quick-tempered teach.

The more flesh [gluttony], the more worms; the more property, the more anxiety; the more schooling, the more wisdom.

Greed and hatred shorten a man's life.

One who is liked by men is liked by God; one who is not liked by men is not liked by God.

Let the honor of your pupil be as dear to you as your own; respect your colleague as you respect your teacher; revere your teacher as you revere God.

Do not try to pacify a friend when he is in a rage; avoid seeing him in the hour of his disgrace.

Knowledge gained when one is young is like ink used on clean, fresh paper; knowledge gained in old age is like ink used on crumpled paper.

He who learns from the young is like one who eats unripe grapes; he who learns from the old is like one who eats ripe grapes or drinks old wine.

Envy, lust and vainglory shorten a man's life.

TALMUD

On Living Wisely

Even a poor man who himself survives on charity should give charity.

TALMUD

I can retract what I did not say, but I cannot retract what I already have said.

SOLOMON IBN GABIROL

Only God can give us credit for the angry words we did not speak.

HAROLD KUSHNER

The tongue is the pen of the heart.

YIDDISH FOLK SAYING

A man must always be considerate of the feelings of his neighbors . . . So, for instance, if I went out to the fair . . . and did well, sold everything at a good profit, and returned with pockets full of money . . . I never failed to tell my neighbors that I had lost every cent and was a ruined man. Thus, I was happy and my neighbors were happy. But if, on the contrary, I had really been cleaned out at the fair . . . I made sure to tell my neighbors that, never since God made fairs, had there been a better one. You get my point? For thus, I was miserable and my neighbors were miserable.

SHALOM ALEICHEM

Remember three things, and you will avoid sin: whence you came, whither you go, and to whom you must account.

AKAVYA BEN MEHALALEL

THREE PROOFS OF WISDOM

A man of Jerusalem with a large sum of money in his possession went into a foreign country on business. In a certain small town he put up at an inn where he had been used to staying. While there, he became seriously ill. So he called the host and entrusted to him all that he had, making him promise to hand it over to his son.

"You will know my son," said the dying man, "by his extraordinary wisdom, which will show that he is indeed my son and not a swindler. Test him on three points of wisdom, and if you are satisfied with the results, give my legacy to him."

The man died, and the news of his death and bequest reached Jerusalem. Meanwhile, the trustee exacted from the people of the town the promise not to give his address to any stranger who might ask about him.

After some time, the son of the deceased man arrived at the place where his father had died. He knew the name of the person with whom his father had usually lodged, but he did not know the man's address, and the people of the town refused to give it to him. In this predicament, he met a man selling wood. This he bought, ordering the woodsman to carry it for him to the house of the man whose address he did not know. On arriving there, the woodsman put down his load.

"What is this?" exclaimed the master of the house; "I have not ordered any wood!"

"True," said the woodsman, "but the young man behind me has." The stranger at once stepped up and made himself known to the master of the house and told him about the trick he had used in order to find him. Pleased with the young man's cleverness, the host invited him to be his guest, and the young Jerusalemite gladly accepted his offer.

Dinner was just then ready. Those sitting at the table consisted of the host, hostess, his two sons, his two daughters and the visitor from Jerusalem. When they were all seated, a dish containing five squabs was placed on the table, and the host asked his guest to serve the portions.

This he did in the following manner: One of the squabs he divided between the host and the hostess, another between the two sons, and a third between the two daughters; the remaining two squabs he took for himself. This strange conduct came as an utter surprise to all of them, but no one commented on it, hoping that the wisdom of it would soon be understood.

At suppertime a fine chicken was placed before the company, and the host again invited the guest to distribute the portions. This he did as follows: The head of the bird he gave to the host, the stuffing to the hostess, a leg to each son, and a wing to each daughter; the remainder he took for himself.

"Sir," said the host at last, "have you any reason for your method of serving? At dinner I thought your method very strange, but now it seems still more extraordinary."

"Have patience with me," replied the Jerusalemite, "and I will explain it all to you. At dinner there were seven of us and only five squabs; as these could not be divided with mathematical exactness, I thought it best to divide them numerically. You and your wife with one squab made three. Your two sons and one squab made another three, and so did your two daughters with one squab. To make up another three, I was obliged to take the other two squabs for myself.

"At supper I was obliged to act on a different principle, according to the altered circumstances. Since you are the head of the family, I gave you the head of the fowl; the inner part of the fowl I gave to your wife, as a sign of her fruitfulness; the legs, symbolic of pillars, I gave to your two sons as the future supporters of your home; the wings that I gave to your daughters were meant to show that they will soon fly away with their husbands; and the body of the fowl which resembles a ship, I kept for myself. In doing this I meant to indicate that as soon as you give me my father's property I shall set sail for home."

These three proofs of wisdom convinced the host that his guest was the rightful heir, and he thereupon handed him his father's legacy and sent him away in peace.

MIDRASH

As You Are

Why did creation begin with a single human being? For the sake of the righteous and the wicked, that none might ascribe their differing characters to hereditary differences. And lest families boast of their high lineage. This they do nonetheless. How much worse it would be if all were not descended from a single source!

TALMUD

Let the world know you as you are, not as you think you should be, because sooner or later, if you are posing, you will forget the pose, and then where are you?

FANNY BRICE

Mistake of a Friend

When a friend makes a mistake, the friend remains a friend, and the mistake remains a mistake.

SHIMON PERES
Commenting on U.S. President Ronald Reagan's visit to the military cemetery in Bitburg, Germany, where Nazi officers were buried.—ed.

In a quarrel, each side is right.

YIDDISH FOLK SAYING

Truth

Justice is truth in action.

BENJAMIN DISRAELI

The Torah will never change, for truth is unchangeable.

JOSEPH ALBO

If anyone tells you that he loves God and does not love his fellow man, you will know that he is lying.

MARTIN BUBER

MUSIC OF THE HEART

The heart, especially the Jewish heart, is a fiddle. You pull strings and out come songs. . . .

SHALOM ALEICHEM

The most direct means for attaching ourselves to God from this material world is through music and song. Even if you can't sing well, sing. Sing to yourself. Sing in the privacy of your own home. But sing.

NACHMAN OF BRATSLAV

SOURCES

Abbot, Lyman. 1835–1922 Preacher and journalist.

Abzug, Bella. 1920–1998. U.S. Congresswoman from New York.

Adams, John. 1735–1826. Second president of the United States (1797–1801)

Adler, E. N. 1861–1946. English author.

Adler, Felix. 1851–1933. Philosopher, educator, and founder of the Ethical Culture Society.

Adler, Herman. 1839–1911. British chief rabbi.

Adler, Morris. 1906–1996. Rabbi, author.

Adler, Rachel. Feminist leader, contemporary author, professor.

Aiken, Lisa. b. 1956. Psychotherapist, lecturer, and author.

Albo, Joseph. 1380–1440. Fifteenth-century Spanish rabbi and philosopher.

Aleichem, Shalom. 1859–1916. Pen name of Sholem Rabinowitz, noted author. Considered the Mark Twain of the Jewish people. His adopted name means "peace be upon you."

Amichai, Yehuda. b. 1924. German-born Israeli poet.

Antin, Mary. 1881–1949. Russian-born American author whose 1912 memoir, *The Promised Land*, was one of the first accounts on the assimilation of European Jews into America.

Arendt, Hannah. 1906–1975. German-born political and social philosopher, and author.

Arens, Moshe. b. 1925. Israeli politician and author.

Arnold, Matthew. 1822–1888. Poet and critic.

Arzt, Max. 1897–1975. U.S. rabbi and author.

Ashe, Arthur. 1943–1993. Tennis player and AIDS activist.

Ba'al Makhshoves. 1873–1924. Pen name of Dr. Israel Eliashov, one of the first Yiddish literary critics.

Ba'al Shem Tov, Israel. 1700–1760. Also known as ben Eliezer, founder of Hasidism.

Balfour, Arthur James. 1848–1930. British statesman and philosopher.

Bock, Jerry. b. 1928. Writer of the musical *Fiddler on the Roof* (1964).

Baeck, Leo. 1873–1956. German rabbi and theologian.

Barry, Patricia Z. Contemporary author.

Begin, Menachem. 1913–1992. Israeli prime minister, 1977–1983.

Beimel, Jacob. 1880–1944. Liturgist and composer of prayer settings. Editor of *The Jewish Music Journal*.

Beit-Hallahmi, Benjamin. b. 1943. Author and Professor at the University of Haifa, Israel.

Bellow, Saul. b. 1915. Author and 1976 Nobel Prize winner for Literature.

Ben-Gurion, David. 1886–1973. First prime minister of Israel (1949–1953); served again as prime minister a second time (1955–1963).

Ben-Yahiel, Asher. Rabbi. 1250–1328. German/Spanish Talmudist.

Berditchevsky, Micha Joseph. Nineteenth-century European scholar and Zionist author.

Berg, Mary B. b. 1926. Polish Jew who lived in the Warsaw Ghetto.

Bernstein, Philip. b. 1901 Twentieth-century rabbi.

Bialik, Chaim Nachman. 1873–1934. Hebrew poet.

Birnbaum, Philip. b. 1904 Polish-born author.

Blumenfeld, Samuel M. 1901–1972. Educator and Zionist. Rabbi.

Bomba, Abraham. (Treblinka) Holocaust survivor.

Bonaparte, Napoléon. 1769–1821 Emperor of France (1804–1815).

Brandeis, Louis D. 1856–1941. U.S. Supreme Court Justice (1916–1939).

Breyer, Stephen G. b. 1938. U.S. Supreme Court Justice (1997–).

Brice, Fanny. 1891–1951. U.S. comedienne and singer.

Buber, Martin. 1878–1965. Jewish philosopher; one of his generation's leading spiritual figures.

Buck, Pearl S. 1892–1973. Novelist.

Cahan, Abraham. 1860–1951. American Yiddish journalist.

Caldwell, Taylor. 1900–1985. Novelist.

Cardin, Nina Beth. b. 1953. Conservative American rabbi.

Chagall, Marc. 1887–1985. Russian-born artist.

Clemens, Samuel L. SEE Mark Twain.

Cohen, David. b. 1955. Writer and editor.

Cohen, Morris Raphael. 1880–1947. Philosopher and professor.

Cohn, David L. 1896–1960. Writer on the subject of American politics and morals.

Coleridge, Samuel Taylor. 1772–1834. British poet and critic.

Collins, Larry, b. 1929. Author.

Cooper, Howard. Contemporary author.

Cowan, Paul. 1940–1988. Rabbi, journalist, and author.

Diamant, Anita. b. 1951. Author.

Davidson, Israel. 1870–1939. Poet, scholar, author.

Dawidowicz, Lucy. 1915–1990. Author, historian, and definitive Holocaust scholar.

Dayan, Moishe. 1915–1981. Chief of staff of the Israeli defense forces in the 1950s; led the Israeli Army to victory in the 1967 Six Day War.

Dershowitz, Alan. b. 1938. Professor, attorney, author.

Disraeli, Benjamin. 1804–1881. British Prime Minister and statesman.

Dobroszycki, Lucjan. 1925–1995. Writer.

Donin, Hayim Halevy. b. 1928. Rabbi and author.

Dubnow, Simon. 1860–1941. Russo-Jewish historian.

Eban, Abba. b. 1915. Israeli diplomat and author.

Einstein, Albert. 1879–1955. German-born physicist and professor. Received the Nobel Prize in 1921 for his theory of relativity.

Eisenberg, Robert. b. 1956. Author.

Elazar, Daniel. b. 1934. Political science professor.

Eliezer, Israel ben. SEE Ba'al Shem Tov.

Elwell, Sue Levi. b. 1948. Rabbi, cofounder of the Los Angeles Jewish Feminist Center.

Fischl, Petr. 1929–1944. Young poet. Died in Auschwitz at age fifteen.

Fleg, Edmond. 1874–1963. French poet and playwright.

Foxman, Abraham. b. 1940. Attorney, author, director of Anti-Defamation League, 1990s.

Frank, Anne. 1929–1945. Dutch citizen and diarist. Her diary is perhaps the most widely read chronicle of the Holocaust.

Frankfurter, Felix. 1882–1965. U.S. Supreme Court Justice (1939–1962).

Freehof, Solomon. 1892–1990. Rabbi and scholar, author and talmudist.

Freespirit, Judy. Contemporary author.

Freud, Sigmund. 1856–1939. Psychiatrist and founder of psychoanalysis.

Friedman, Barry. b. 1934. Reform rabbi, author.

Friedmann, Pavel. 1921–1944. Young Czech poet. Lived in Therezin Ghetto, died in Auschwitz.

Fuchs, Alan D. b. 1936. Reform rabbi.

Gabirol, Solomon Ibn. c. 1022–c. 1070. Spanish Jew, poet, and philosopher.

Geller, Laura. b. 1950. Rabbi, the third woman ordained through the reform movement.

Ginsburg, Ruth Bader. b. 1933. U.S. Supreme Court Justice.

Glazer, Richard. Holocaust Survivor.

Gold, Herbert. b. 1924. Novelist.

Golden, Harry. 1903–1981. Journalist and author.

Goldman, Ari. b. 1949. Journalist and professor of religion.

Goldstein, Albert S. b. 1908. Rabbi, author.

Gorky, Maxim. 1868–1936. Pen name of Aleksey M. Peshkov, Russian man of letters.

Gottheil, Gustav. 1827–1903. Reform Rabbi, German philosopher.

Green, Arthur. b. 1941 Rabbi, professor.

Greenberg, Blu. b. 1936. Essayist on roles of women in traditional Judaism.

Greenberg, Louis. 1894–1946. Writer.

Grossberg, Shlomit. b. 1960s. Young Jewish poet.

Ha'am, Ahad. 1856–1927. Pseudonym of Asher Ginzberg, Ukranian-born essayist, philosopher.

Harkavy, Alexander. 1863–1939. Writer.

Harnick, Sheldon. b. 1924 Writer of the musical *Fiddler on the Roof* (1964).

Hausner, Gideon. 1915–1990. Israeli lawyer and prosecutor of Karl Adolf Eichmann (1961).

Heine, Heinrich. 1797–1856. German poet and critic.

Herford, Robert Travers. 1860–1950. Author.

Hertz, Joseph H. 1872–1946. Chief Rabbi of England, author.

Herzl, Theodor. 1860–1904. Founder of the Political Zionist movement.

Heschel, Abraham Joshua. 1907–1972. Rabbi, theologian, activist, and author.

Hillel the Elder. 1st century B.C.—1st century A.D. Jewish scholar in Palestine.

Hirsch, Emil G. 1851–1923. Reform Rabbi.

Holmes, Oliver Wendell. 1809–1894. Poet, essayist, physician.

Howe, Irving. 1920–1993. Literary critic, professor, and author.

Imber, Naphtali Herz. 1856–1909. Hebrew poet.

Jabotinsky, Vladimir. 1880–1940. Russian-born Jew and Zionist; founder of the Revisionists.

Joseph, Morris. 1848–1930. British Rabbi.

Jung, Leo. 1876–1949. Rabbi and author.

Kallen, Horace. 1882–1974. American philosopher.

Kaplan, Mordecai M. 1881–1983 Rabbi, founder of Reconstructionist movement.

Kaplan, Sylvia R. Author.

Katznelson, Yitzchak. b. ?–1944. French citizen and poet. Died in Auschwitz.

Kazin, Alfred. 1915–1998. Author, editor, literary critic.

Klagsbrun, Francine. b. 1931. Writer and lecturer on family, social change, ethics, and feminism.

Kolitz, Zvi. b. 1913. Israeli-born, U.S. essayist, journalist, teacher at Yeshiva University.

Kompert, Leopold. 1822–1886. German-Austrian writer.

Kook, Abraham Isaac. 1865–1935. Chief Rabbi of Palestine.

Kosek, Miroslav. 1932–1944. Young poet. Died in Auschwitz at age twelve.

Kushner, Harold. b. 1935. Conservative Rabbi and author.

Kushner, Larry. b. 1943. Author and Reform Rabbi.

Lapierre, Dominick. Contemporary author.

Lazarus, Emma. 1849–1887. American-born poet.

Leitner, Isabella. b. 1924. Author.

Lelyveld, Arthur. 1913–1996. Reform Rabbi.

Levenson, Sam. 1914–1980. Comedian and author.

Levi, Shonie. b. 1907. Author.

Lipstadt, Deborah E. b. 1947. Historian, noted Holocaust scholar, and author.

Lloyd George, David. 1863–1945. British Prime Minister (1916–1922).

Longfellow, Henry W. 1807–1882. Poet.

Macaulay, Lord. 1800–1891. British historian, essayist and politician.

Maimonides, Moses. 1135–1204. Also known as Moses ben Maimon, the RamBam. Spanish Rabbi, physician, scholar, talmudist, philosopher, and court-physician. His major work was the *Mishne Torah*, a summary of Jewish law.

Mawult, Jan. Polish Jew who lived in the Warsaw Ghetto.

Meir, Golda. 1898–1978. Milwaukee schoolteacher who became prime minister of Israel (1969–1974).

Mennis, Bernice. Contemporary author.

Miller, Judith. b. 1948. Journalist and author.

Mittlestein, Rachel. b. circa 1890. Author.

Montague, Lily H. 1873–1963. British social worker and religious leader.

Montefiore, Claude G. 1858–1938. British scholar, theologian, and lay preacher.

Morais, Sabato. 1823–1897. Rabbi, Sephardic Jew.

Moskowitz, Faye. b. 1930. Author.

Nachman, Rebbe, of Bratzlav. 1772–1810 Hasidic Rabbi, great grandson of Rabbi Israel Ba'al Shem Tov, founder of the Hasidic movement.

Nietzsche, Friedrich. 1844–1900. German philosopher.

Novotney, Ann. Contemporary writer of stories about the American immigrant.

O'Connor, John Cardinal. 1920–2000. Catholic prelate, New York Cardinal.

Ogen, Rachel. b. 1927. Polish-born Israeli Palmach member.

Ornstein, Anna. b. 1927. Holocaust survivor, psychologist.

Ostriker, Alicia. b. 1937. Author.

Oz, Amos. b. 1939. Israeli essay and fiction writer, activist.

Ozick, Cynthia. b. 1928 Novelist and essayist, poet and critic.

Paley, Grace. b. 1922 Writer and peace activist, novelist, essayist, political reporter.

Peshkov, Aleksey M. SEE Maxim Gorky.

Pogrebin, Letty Cottin. b. 1939. Founding editor of *Ms.* magazine, columnist, feminist, political activist, and author.

Potok, Chaim. b. 1929. Rabbi, novelist, and historian.

Prose, Francine. b. 1947. Author.

Rabin, Yitzhak. 1922–1995. Soldier, Israeli Prime Minister in the 1970s, Defense Minister in the 1980s, and Prime Minister in 1992.

Rackman, Emanuel. b. 1910. Orthodox rabbi and scholar.

Rashi. 1041–1105. Shlomo Yitz°haqi. Talmudic commentator, translations still in use today.

Raskin, Philip M. 1880–1944. Russian-born poet, Zionist, and lecturer.

Ravage, Marcus. 1884–1965. Writer.

Reich, Walter. b. 1943. Journalist and author.

Riemer, Jack. b. 1929. Rabbi and author.

Reimers, Paula. b. 1947. Rabbi, converted to Judaism in 1981.

Reyner, John. Noted liberal British rabbi.

Riziner Rebbe. Eighteenth-century Hasidic Rabbi.

Roiphe, Anne. b. 1935. Novelist and nonfiction writer.

Roosevelt, Franklin Delano. 1882–1945. Thirty-second President of the United States (1933–1945).

Roosevelt, Theodore. 1858–1919. b. 1945 Twenty-sixth President of the United States (1901–1909).

Rosen, Jonathan. b. 1963. Author.

Rosenfeld, Morris. 1862–1923. Yiddish poet.

Rosenfeld, Oskar. 1884–1944. Polish Jew who lived in the Warsaw Ghetto.

Rosh. 1250–1327. Rabbi Asher ben Jehiel.

Rosten, Leo. 1908–1997. Yiddishist and humor writer.

Rotblit, Yahacob. b. 1945. Twentieth-century Israeli poet and songwriter.

Roth, Philip. b. 1933. Author and Pulitzer Prize winner.

Rothschild, Baron Lionel de. 1808–1879. First Jewish member of Parliament and leader of Anglo-Jewish community.

Rothchild, Sylvia Helen. b. 1923. Rabbi and author.

Rukeyser, Muriel. b. 1913. Poet and author.

Sachar, Abram Leon. 1899–1993. Historian and educator.

Sacks, Jonathan. b. 1948. Author. Current chief rabbi of Great Britain.

Salisbury, Harrison. b. 1908. Journalist and Pulitzer Prize winner, 1955.

Salkin, Jeffrey. b. 1954. Rabbi and author.

Samuel, Maurice. 1895–1972. Romanian-born writer.

Sasso, Sandy Eisenberg. b. 1947. Reconstrutionist Rabbi and author.

Schechter, Solomon. 1850–1915. Theologian, Talmudist, and essayist. Founder of the Conservative movement.

Schindler, Alexander M. 1925–2000. Noted Reform Rabbi, preeminent figure of conscience and leadership around the globe.

Schweitzer, Albert. 1875–1965. German Philosopher, winner of the Nobel Peace Prize, 1952.

Seidman, Hillel. b. 1915. Author.

Senesh, Hannah. 1921–1944. Hungarian-born poet and heroine.

Serhan, Gassoub. b. circa 1950. Young Arab from village of Kfar Yafia.

Shamir, Yitzak. b. 1915. Polish-born foreign minister of Israel, (1980–1983); prime minister of Israel (1983–1984, 1986–1992).

Sharansky, Natan. b. 1948. Ukranian-born Zionist who brought sympathy to the Soviet Jewish cause. After nine years in Russian prison, became Israeli minister of commerce and industry in June 1996.

Shaw, George Bernard. 1856–1950. Irish dramatist and man of letters.

Shimoni, Yaacov. b. 1915. Israeli writer specializing in the Middle East.

Shostakovich, Dmitry. 1906–1975. Russian composer.

Siegel, Hassia. b. 1920s. European-born, American Yiddish teacher.

Silver, Abba Hillel. 1893–1963. Rabbi and Zionist leader. Reform movement leader in early part of twentieth century.

Silverberg, Robert. b. 1935. Author.

Singer, Issac Bashevis. 1904–1991. Polish-born novelist, 1978 Nobel Prize winner.

Sirkin, Dr. Marie. b. 1900. Writer.

Slomninsky, Henry. b. 1884–1970. Contemporary philosopher.

Stevenson, Robert Louis. 1850–1894. Poet, essayist, and novelist.

Straus, Oscar S. 1850–1926. U.S. statesman.

Tarr, Herbert. 1929–1993. Author.

Telushkin, Joseph b. 1948. Rabbi and author.

Tolstoy, Leo. 1828–1910. Russian novelist and social reformer.

Tomashevsky, Leah. b. 1980s. Dartmouth student, former intern at U.S. Holocaust Memorial Museum, Washington, D.C.

Twain, Mark. Pen name of Samuel L. Clemens. 1835–1910. Noted American writer, lecturer, and humorist.

Villard, Oswald Garrison. 1872–1942. Writer and editor.

Voltaire, F.M.A. 1694–1778. French philosopher and man of letters.

Washington, George. 1732–1799. First President of the United States (1789–1797).

Webster, Daniel. 1782–1852. Politician and U.S. secretary of state.

Weinberg, Sydney Stahl. b. 1938. Author.

Weiss-Rosmarin, Trude. 1908–1989. German-born publisher, author, and lecturer.

Weizmann, Chaim. 1874–1952. Russian-born chemist, Zionist leader, first president of Israel (1948–1952).

Whitehead, Alfred North. 1861–1947. British Philosopher and mathematician.

Wiesel, Elie. b. 1928. Rumanian-born author, Holocaust scholar, professor, winner of the 1986 Nobel Peace Prize.

Wilson, Woodrow. 1856–1924. Twenty-eighth President of the United States (1913–1921).

Wise, Rabbi Stephen S. 1874–1949. U.S. Rabbi, Zionist leader, and educator.

Wouk, Herman. b. 1915. Author, winner of the Pulitzer Prize in 1952.

Yezierska, Anzia. 1885–1970. Russian-born novelist who wrote from experience about American immigrants and the sweatshops.

Zabara, Joseph. Twelfth-century writer.

Zangwill, Israel. 1864–1926. Novelist and playwright.

Zimmerman, Bonnie. b. 1947. Author.

Zola, Émile. 1840–1902. French writer.

BIBLIOGRAPHY

Abbot, Lyman. In *Light from Jewish Lamps, A Modern Treasury of Jewish Thoughts*. Editor Sidney Greenberg. Northvale, NJ: Jason Aronson, Inc., 1986.

Abzug, Bella. In *Great Jewish Quotations*. Editor, Alfred J. Kolatch. New York: Jonathan David, 1996.

—"Bella on Bella" in *American Jewish Woman: A Documentary History*. Editor, Jacob Rade Cincinnati: KTAV Publishing house, American Jewish Archives, 1981.

Adams, John. "John Adams to F. A. Van Der Kemp, 16 February 1809." In *What Did They Think of the Jews?* Editor, Allan Gould. Northvale, NJ: Jason Aaronson Inc., 1991.

Adler, Felix. "The Revival of Anti-Semitism" from *The Standard*. New York City. January, 1921.

Adler, Morris. In *Light from Jewish Lamps, A Modern Treasury of Jewish Thoughts*. Editor, Sidney Greenberg. Northvale, NJ: Jason Aronson, Inc., 1986.

Adler, Rachel. *Lilith Magazine*, Winter 1976–77.

Ahad Ha-am. In *Ahad Ha-am: Essays, Letters, and Memoirs*. Leon, Simon, 1946.

Aiken, Lisa. *To Be A Jewish Woman*. Lisa Aiken, Pub.

Aleichem, Shalom. In Klagsbrun, Francine, *Voices of Wisdom: Jewish Ideals and Ethics for Everyday Living*. New York: Pantheon Books, 1980.

—*World of Sholem Aleichem*. Maurice Samuel. New York: Knopf, 1943.

—*From the Fair: An autobiography of Sholem Aleichem*. Curt Levitant. New York: Viking Penguin, 1985.

Amichai, Yehuda. *Poems of Jerusalem*. New York: Harper and Row, 1988.

—"My Father's Memorial Day," from *Amen*, New York: Harper and Row, 1977.

Anielewicz, Mordecai. *Great Jewish Quotations*. Editor, Alfred J. Kolatch. New York: Jonathan David, 1996.

Antin, Mary. *The Promised Land*. Cambridge, Boston and New York: The Riverside Press/Houghton Mifflin Company, 1912.

Arens, Moshe. In *Moshe Arens: Statesman and Scientist Speaks Out*. Merrill, Simon. Middle Island, NY: Dean Books, 1988.

Arnold, Matthew. "Literature and Dogma," in *What Did They Think of the Jews*. Editor, Allan Gould. Northvale, NJ: Jason Aaronson, Inc., 1991.

Ashe, Arthur and Arnold Rampersad. *Days of Grace*. New York: Alfred A. Knopf, 1993.

Ba'al Makhshoves. In *Voices from the Yiddish*. Editor, Irving Howe and Eliezer Greenberg, Ann Arbor: University of Michigan Press, 1972.

Baal Shem Tov, Israel. In *Living a Jewish Life*. Diamant, Anita and Howard Cooper. New York: Harper Perennial, 1991.

Baeck, Leo. *The Essence of Judaism*. New York: Schocken Books, 1936.

Barry, Patricia Z. In *Wrestling with the Angels: Jewish Insights on Death and Mourning*. Editor, Jack Riemer. New York: Schocken Books, 1995.

Begin, Menachem. In *Great Jewish Quotations*. Editor, Alfred J. Kolatch. New York: Jonathan David, 1996.

Beit-Hallahmi, Benjamin. *Original Sins: Reflections on the History of Zionism and Israel*. Brooklyn, NY: Olive Branch Press, 1993.

Bellow, Saul. *To Jerusalem and Back: A Personal Account*. New York: Viking Press, 1976.

Ben-Yahiel, Asher. In *New Treasury of Judaism*. Editor, Philip Birnbaum. New York: Hebrew Publishing Company, 1977.

Berg, Mary B. In *In the Warsaw Ghetto: Summer 1941*. New York: Aperture Foundation, Inc., 1993.

Bernstein, Phillip. From the forward of *Tzedakah: A Way of Life*. Editor, Azriel Eisenbeg. New Jersey: Behrman House, 1963.

Beimel, Jacob. "Divinity and Music: a Jewish Conception," in *The Jewish Music Journal*. July, 1934.

Birnbaum, Philip. *New Treasury of Judaism*. New York: Hebrew Publishing Company, 1977.

Blumenfeld, Samuel. In *Light from Jewish Lamps, A Modern Treasury of Jewish Thoughts*. Editor, Sidney Greenberg. Northvale, NJ: Jason Aronson, Inc., 1986.

Bomba, Abraham. In *Shoah: An Oral History of the Holocaust*. Editor, Claude Lanzmann. New York: Pantheon Books, 1985.

Brandeis, Justice Louis D. In *Lights from Jewish Lamps, A Modern Treasury of Jewish Thoughts*. Editor, Sidney Greenberg. Northvale, NJ: Jason Aronson, Inc., 1986.

—From an address, April 22, 1904. In *The Judaic Tradition*. Editor, Nahum Glatzer. Boston: Beacon Press, 1969.

Breyer, Stephen G. In Elinor and Robert Slater's *Great Jewish Men*. Middle Village, NY: Johnathan David, Publisher, 1996.

Brice, Fanny. In Norman Katkov's *Fabulous Fanny: the Story of Fanny Brice*. New York: Knopf, 1953.

Buber, Martin. *Ten Rungs: Hasidic Sayings*. New York: Shocken, 1947.

—*Zion and Youth*, 1918.

Buck, Pearl. In *Lights from Jewish Lamps, A Modern Treasury of Jewish Thoughts*. Editor, Sidney Greenberg. NJ: Jason Aronson, Inc., Northvale, 1986.

Cardin, Nina Beth. In *Jewish Woman's Book of Wisdom*. Editor, Ellen Jaffe-Gill. New Jersey: Birch Lane Press, 1998.

Chagall, Marc. Speech at opening of Hadassah, Hospital, Jerusalem, Israel.

Churchill, Sir Winston. In Benjamin Netanyahu's *A Place Among the Nations*, New York: Bantam Books, 1993.

Cohen, David. *Jews in America*. San Francisco: Collins Publishers, 1967/1989.

Cohn, David. "I've Kept My Name." *The Atlantic Monthly*. April, 1948.

Cohen, Morris Raphael. *A Dreamer's Journey*. Boston: Beacon Press, 1949.

Collins, Larry and Dominique LaPierre. *Oh, Jerusalem*. New York: Simon and Schuster, 1972.

Cowan, Paul. *An Orphan In History: Retrieving a Jewish Legacy*. New York: Doubleday, 1982.

Davidson, Israel. In *Out of Endless Yearnings: A Memoir of Israel Davidson*. C. Davidson. Bloch Publishing, 1946.

Dawidowicz, Lucy. *From that Place and Time: A Memoir 1938–1947*. New York: W. W. Norton and Company.

Dayan, Moishe. *Living with the Bible*. New York: William Morrow, 1978.

—In *Original Sins: Reflections on the History of Zionism and Israel*. Editor, Benjamin Beit-Hallahmi. Brooklyn NY: Olive Branch Press, an imprint of Interlink Publishing Group, Inc., 1993.

Dershowitz, Alan. *The Vanishing American Jew: In Search of Jewish Identity of the Next Century*. Boston: Little Brown and Company, 1997.

Diamant, Anita and Howard Cooper. *Living a Jewish Life*. New York: Harper Perrenial, 1991.

Disraeli, Benjamin. From a February 11, 1851 speech.

Herman Hertz, Joseph. *A Book of Jewish Thoughts*. New York: Bloch Publishers, 1954.

Donin, Hayim Halevy. *To Pray as a Jew*. New York: Basic Books, 1980.

Dubnow, Simon. In *Great Jewish Quotations*. Editor, Alfred J. Kolatch. New York: Jonathan David, 1996.

Eban, Abba. From a 1952 address.

Einstein, Albert. *The World as I See It*. New York: New York Philosophical Library, 1945.

Eisenberg, Robert. *Boychicks in the Hood—Travels in the Hasidic Underground*. San Francisco: Harper Collins, 1995.

Elazar, Daniel. *American Jewish Yearbook* (1969). Philadelphia: American Jewish Committee, 1969.

Eliezer, Israel Ben. The Baal Shem Tov. In *Living a Jewish Life*, Anita Damiant and Howard Cooper. New York: Harper Perennial, 1991.

Elwell, Sue Levi. "Rosh Hashanah Sermon 24 Sept. 1987," *Four Centuries of Jewish Women's Spirituality*. Editors, Ellen Umansky and Dianne Ashton. Boston: Beacon Press, 1992.

Fischl, Petr. In *I Never Saw Another Butterfly: Children's Drawings and Poems from Terezin Concentration Camp 1942–1944*. New York: Schocken Books, 1978.

Fleg, Edmond. "I Am A Jew" in *Why I Am a Jew: The Modern Jewish Experience*. New York: Arno Press, 1975.

—*The Jewish Anthology*. Translated by Maurice Samuel. New Jersey: Behrman House, 1933.

Foxman, Abraham. In an address to the World Conference on Anti-Semitism and Prejudice in a Changing World, Brussels, Belgium, July 1992.

Frank, Anne. *The Diary of Anne Frank: The Critical Edition*. New York: Doubleday, 1952.

Freehof, Solomon. *From a Small Sanctuary*. Cincinnati: Union of American Hebrew Congregations, 1942.

Freespirit, Judy. In *The Tribe of Dina: A Jewish Women's Anthology*. Editors, Melanie Kaye/Kantrowitz and Irena Klepfisz. Boston: Beacon Press, 1986, 1989.

Freud, Sigmund. *Psychoanalytical Quarterly. 1942*.

Friedan Betty Naomi. *New York Times Magazine*, October 28, 1984.

Friedman, Barry. *New Light Siddur*. Livingston, NJ: Temple B'nai Abraham, 1991.

Friedmann, Pavel. "I Never Saw Another Butterfly," in *I Never Saw Another Butterfly—Children's Drawings and Poems from Terezin Concentration Camp 1942–1944*. New York: Schocken Books, 1978.

Fuchs, Rabbi Alan D. "From Wise to Wisdom" from a speech at Temple Emanuel, New York City, November 11, 2000.

Geller, Laura. In *On Being a Jewish Feminist*. Editor, Susannah Heschel. New York: Schocken books, 1983.

George, David Lloyd. "What Has the Jew Done?" in *Zionism and Anti-Semitism: The Absurd Folly of Jew-Baiting*. New York: American Jewish Congress, 1923.

Ginsberg, Ruth Bader. "What Being Jewish Means to Me," in *The Journey Home, Jewish Women and the American Century*, by Joyce Antler. New York: The Free Press, 1997.

—"Being Jewish Today," *The New York Times*, Jan. 14, 1996.

Glatzer, Nahum. *The Judaic Tradition*. Boston: Beacon Press, 1969.

—*The Language of Faith*. New York: Shocken, 1967.

Gold, Herbert. *My Last Two Thousand Years*. New York: Random House, 1972.

Goldberg, Arthur J. at his inauguration as U.S. Ambassador to the United Nations on July 26, 1965.

Goldman, Ari. *The Search for God at Harvard*. New York: Times Books, 1991.

Gordon, Aaron David. In Ernst Harthern's *Going Home*. Indianapolis: Bobbs-Merrill, 1938.

Gorky, Maxim. In *Light from Jewish Lamps, A Modern Treasury of Jewish Thoughts*. Editor, Sidney Greenberg. Northvale, NJ: Jason Aronson, Inc., 1986.

Gottheil, Gustav. English adaptation of German *Chanukah* hymn.

Green, Arthur. "Sheckihanah" from *On being a Jewish Feminist*. Editor, Susannah Heschel. New York: Schocken Books, 1995.

Greenberg, Blu. *How to Run a Traditional Jewish Household*. New York: Simon and Shuster, 1983.

Greenberg, Louis. *The Jews in Russia*, vol. I. New Haven, CT: Yale University Press, 1944.

Grossberg, Shlomit. In *My Shalom, My Peace: Paintings and Poems by Jewish and Arab Children*. Editor, Jacob Zim and Uriel Ofek. The American Israel Publishing Co., Ltd. and Sonol Israel, Ltd., 1975.

Harkavy, Alexander. In *American Jewish Album: 1654 to the Present*. Editor, Allon Schoener. New York: Rizzoli International, 1983.

Hausner, Gideon. In *Judaic Tradition*. Editor, Nahum Glatzer. Boston: Beacon Press, 1969.

Hertz, Joseph Herman. *A Book of Jewish Thoughts*. New York: Bloch Publishers, 1954.

Herzl, Theodor. *The Jewish State*. The manifesto of the Zionist movement, 1896.

—Zion and Youth (1918).

Heschel, Abraham Joshua. In *The Wisdom of Heschel*. Editor, Rita Goodhill. New York: Farrar, Straus and Giroux, 1975.

—*Man's Quest for God*. New York: Scribner and Sons, 1954.

—*Man Is Not Alone*. New York: Farrar, Straus and Giroux, 1976.

Hirsch, Emil G. In *A Book of Jewish Thoughts*, Joseph Herman Hertz. New York: Bloch Publishers, 1954.

Holmes, Oliver Wendel. *Over the Teacups. 1891.*

Howe, Irving and Eliezer Greenberg. *Voices from the Yiddish*. Ann Arbor: University of Michigan Press, 1972.

—*World of Our Fathers*. New York and London: Harcourt Brace Jovanovich, 1976.

Jung Leo. "Between Man and Man" in *New Treasury of Judaism*. Editor, Philip Birnbaum. New York: Hebrew Publishing Co., 1977.

Kaplan, Mordecai M. *Not So Random Thoughts*. New York: Reconstructionist Press, 1966.

—*The Meaning of God in Modern Jewish Religion*. Detroit: Wayne State University Press, 1994.

Kallen, Horace. In *Jewish Writer in America: The Assimilation and the Crisis of Identity*. Editor, Allen Guttmann. Oxford University Press, Inc., 1971.

Katzenelson, Yitzchak. *The Song of the Murdered Jewish People*, translated and annotated by Noah Rosenbloom. Beit Lohamei Haghetaot, Tel Aviv Hakibbutz Hameuchad Publishing, 1980.

Kazin, Alfred. *A Walker in the City*. New York: Grove Press, 1951.

Kompert, Leopold. In *Book of Jewish Thoughts*, Joseph Herman Hertz. New York: Bloch Publishers, 1954.

A. I. Kook. In *The Zionist Idea: A Historical Analysis and Reader*. Editor, Arthur Hertzberg. Philadelphia: Jewish Publication Society, 1997.

Kosek, Miroslav. In *I Never Saw Another Butterfly—Children's Drawings and Poems from Terezin Concentration Camp 1942–1944*. New York: Schocken Books, 1978.

Kushner, Harold. *When All You've Ever Wanted Isn't Enough*. New York: Summit Books, 1986.

—*To Life!* Boston: Little Brown, 1993.

Kushner, Lawrence. In *Living a Jewish Life*. Editors, Anita Diamant and Howard Cooper. New York: Harper Perennial, 1991.

Lazarus, Emma. Poem inscribed on the base of the Statue of Liberty, New York City.

Leitner, Isabella. *Fragments of Isabella*. New York: New American Library, 1985.

Levenson, Sam. *Everything But Money*. New York: Simon and Schuster, Inc., 1966.

Lipstadt, Deborah. "And Deborah Made Ten" from *On Being a Jewish Feminist*. Editor, Susannah Heschel. New York: Schocken Books, 1983.

Mawult, Jan. *In the Warsaw Ghetto: Summer 1941*. Editor, Raphael Scharf. Aperture Foundation Inc., 1993.

Mennis, Bernice. In *The Tribe of Dina: A Jewish Women's Anthology*. Editors, Melanie Kaye/Kantrowitz and Irena Klepfisz. Boston: Beacon Press, 1986, 1989.

Meir, Golda. *Land of our Own: An Oral Autobiography*. Editor, Marie Syrkin. New York: Putnam, 1973.

Miller, Judith. *One by One by One: Facing the Holocaust*. New York: Simon and Schuster, 1990.

Mittlestein, Rachel. In *The World of Our Mothers*. Editor, Sydney Stahl Weinberg. Chapel Hill and London: University of North Carolina Press, 1988.

Montague, Lily H. In *Great Jewish Women*. Editors, Eleanor and Robert Slater. Middle Village, NY: Jonathan David, 1994.

Montefiore, Claude G. In *A Book of Jewish Thoughts*. Editor, Joseph Herman Hertz. New York: Bloch Publishers, 1954.

Morais, Sabato. In *LightfromJewishLamps, AModernTreasuryofJewishThoughts*. Editor, SidneyGreenberg. Northvale, NJ: JasonAronson, Inc, 1986.

Moskowitz, Faye. *A Leak in the Heart: Tales From A Woman's Life*. Boston: David R. Godine, 1985.

Nachman, Rebbe, of Bratzlav. *The Empty Chair—Finding Hope and Joy, Timeless Wisdom from a Hasidic Master*. Woodstock, VT: Jewish Lights Publishing, 1994.

Nietzsche, Friedrich. *Beyond Good and Evil*. Translated by Walther Kaufman. New York: Random house, 1989.

Nordau, Max. In *Original Sins: Reflections on the History of Zionism and Israel*. Editor, Benjamin Beit-Hallahmi. Brooklyn, NY: Interlink Publishing Group, 1993.

Novotney, Ann. In *Jews of America*. Editor, Francis Butwin. New Jersey: Behrman house, 1969/1973.

O'Connor, John Cardinal. In *The New York Times*. Sept 19, 1999.

Ogen, Rachel. In *Testament: At the Creation of the State of Israel*. Editor, Aaron Levin. New York: Artisan, 1998.

Ornstein, Anna. In *Generation Without Memory*, Anne Roiphe. New York: Linden Press, Simon and Schuster, 1981.

Ostriker, Alicia. In *People of the Book: Thirty Scholars Reflect on Their Jewish Identity*. Editor, Jeffrey Rubin-Dorsky and Shelly Fisher-Fishkin. Madison WI: University of Wisconsin Press, 1996.

Oz, Amos. In *Testament—At the Creation of the State of Israel*. Editor, Aaron Levin. New York: Artisan, 1998.

Cynthia Ozick. "Notes Toward Finding the Right Question" from *The Tribe of Dina—A Jewish Women's Anthology*. Editors, Melanie Kaye/Kantrowitz and Irena Klepfisz. Boston: Beacon Press, 1986, 1989.

—In *Cynthia Ozick's Fiction*. Editor, Elaine Kauvar. Bloomington: Indiana Press, 1993.

Paley, Grace. *Just As I Thought*. New York: Farrar, Straus, Giroux, 1998.

Peres, Shimon. In *Great Jewish Quotations*. Editor, Alfred J. Kolatch. New York: Jonathan David, 1996.

Pogrebin, Letty Cottin. *Deborah, Golda and Me*, New York: Crown, 1991.

—"Confessions of a Contradictory Jew," *National Council of Jewish Woman Journal*, Spring 1998.

Potok, Chaim. From the Introduction in *Jews in America*. Editor, David Cohen. San Francisco: Collins Publishers, 1989.

Prose, Francine. In *The Jewish Writer*. Editor, Jill Krementz. New York: Henry Holt, 1998.

Rabin, Yitzhak. In *Great Jewish Quotations*. Editor, Alfred J. Kolatch. New York: Jonathan David, 1996.

Rackman, Emanuel. In *Light from Jewish Lamps, A Modern Treasury of Jewish Thoughts*. Editor, Sidney Greenberg. Northvale, NJ: Jason Aronson, Inc., 1986.

Raskin, Philip M. *Songs of a Wanderer*. Philadelphia: Jewish Publication Society of America, 1917.

Ravage, Marcus. In *World of Our Fathers*. Editor, Irving Howe. New York and London: Harcourt Brace Jovanovich, 1976.

Reimer, Jack. *Wrestling with the Angels: Jewish Insights on Death and Mourning*. New York: Schocken Books, 1995.

Reimers, Rabbi Paula. "Mikveh Journal," in *Lechem Tafayal, the Student Journal of The Jewish Theological Seminary*. Editor, David Seindenberg, vol. 1, issue 1, Winter 1990.

Roiphe, Anne. *Generation Without Memory*. New York: Linden Press, Simon and Schuster, 1981.

Roosevelt, Franklin D. In *Light from Jewish Lamps, A Modern Treasury of Jewish Thoughts*. Editor, Sidney Greenberg. Northvale, NJ: Jason Aronson, Inc., 1986.

Roosevelt, Theodore. *Theodore Roosevelt: an Autobiography*. New York: Charles Scribner's Sons, 1922.

Rosen, Jonathan. *The Talmud and the Internet*. New York: Farrar, Straus, Giroux, 2000.

Rosenfeld, Oskar. *Chronicle of the Lodz Ghetto; 1941–1944*. Editor, Lucian Dobroszycki, translated by Richard Lourie. New Haven: Yale University Press, 1984.

Rosten, Leo. *Treasury of Jewish Quotations*. New York: McGraw-Hill, 1972.

Roth, Philip. *The Facts: A novelist's autobiography*. New York: Farrar, Straus, Giroux, 1988.

—*Portnoy's Complaint*. New York: Random House, 1969.

—*Patrimony*. New York: Simon and Schuster, 1991.

Rothchild, Sylvia Helen. *Voices from the Holocaust*. New York: New American Library, 1981.

Sachar, Abram Leon. *A History of the Jews*. New York: Knopf, 1930.

Sacks, Jonathan. *Will We Have Jewish Grandchildren? Jewish Continuity and How to Achieve It*. Portland, OR: Vallentine Mitchell, 1994.

Salisbury, Harrison. *Journey for Our Times: A Memoir*. New York: Harper and Row, 1983.

Salkin, Rabbi Jeffrey. *Putting God on the Guest List*. Woodstock, VT: Jewish Lights, 1993.

Samuel, Maurice. *World of Sholom Aleichem*. New York: Knopf, 1943.

Sasso, Sandy Eisenberg. In *Putting God on the Guest List,* Jeffrey Salkin. Woodstock, VT: Jewish Lights, 1993.

—Adoption prayer from *A Ceremonies Sampler*. Editor, Elizabeth Resnick Levine. La Jolla, CA: Woman's Institute for Continuing Jewish Education.

Schindler, Alexander M. *Hear God's Call: A Communal Ethical Will,* from the Presidential address to the Union of American Hebrew Congregations. December 2, 1995.

—"God and the Holocaust." Address at CLAL conference on Jewish Unity Princeton, New Jersey March 16, 1986. Holocaust Commemorative Program April 7, 1999.

Seidman, Hillel. *Blessed is the Daughter*. Meyer Waxman Shengold books, a division of Schreiber Publishing, Rockville, MD 1959.

Senesch, Hannah. *Hannah Senesh, Her Life & Diary*. New York: Schocken Books, 1973.

Serhan, Gassoub. In *My Shalom, My Peace*. The American Israel Publishing Co., Ltd. and Sonol Israel Ltd., 1975.

Shamir, Itzak. *Summing Up: An Autobiography of Itzak Shamir*. New York: Little Brown, 1994.

Sharansky, Natan. Statement to a Moscow court before being sentenced on July 14, 1978, in *Great Jewish Quotations*. Editor, Alfred J. Kolatch New York: Jonathan David, 1996.

Shostakovich, Dmitri. *Testimony, The Memoirs of Dmitri Shostakovich*. Editor, Solomon Vlokov. New York: Harper and Row, 1979.

Siegel, Hassia. From a conversation with the author, 1998.

Silver, Rabbi Abba Hillel. In *Light from Jewish Lamps, A Modern Treasury of Jewish Thoughts*. Editor, Sidney Greenberg. Northvale, NJ: Jason Aronson, Inc., 1986.

Silverberg, Robert. *If I Forget Thee, O Jerusalem*. New York: Wm. Morrow and Co., 1970.

Singer, Issac Bashevis. In *Dialogues in Judaism—Jewish Dilemmas Defined, Debated and Explored*. Editor, William Berkowitz. Northvale, NJ: Jason Aronson, Inc., 1991.

Sirkin, Dr. Marie. In *Dialogues in Judaism—Jewish Dilemmas Defined, Debated and Explored*. Editor, William Berkowitz. Northvale, NJ: Jason Aronson, Inc., 1991.

Slomninsky, Henry. "Gates of Prayer" originally published under the title "Prayer" in *The Jewish Teacher,* February 1965.

Stein, Sharon. "Envied the kibbutz and set fire to the wheat" in *Original Sins: Reflections on the History of Zionism and Israel*. Editor, Benjamin Beit-Hallahmi. Brooklyn, NY: Olive Branch Press, 1993.

Tarr, Herbert. *Conversion of Chaplain Cohen*. New York: Random House, 1963.

Telushkin, Joseph. *Jewish Wisdom*. New York: William Morrow and Company, 1994.

Tomashevsky, Leah. Conversation with the author, July, 1999.

Tolstoy, Leo. In *Der Israelit* of Frankfurt am Main.

Twain, Mark. "Concerning the Jews" in *Harper's Magazine*, June 1899.

Villard, Oswald Garrison. *Fighting Years, Memoirs of a Liberal Editor*. New York: Harcourt, Brace, 1939.

Washington, George. Public Correspondence, 17 August, 1790.

Webster, Daniel. Private Correspondence, vol. II, in *What Did They Think of the Jews*. Editor, Allan Gould. Northvale NJ: Jason Aronson Inc, 1991.

Weinberg, Sidney. *World of Our Mothers*. Chapel Hill and London: University of North Carolina Press, 1988.

Weiss-Rosmarin, Trude. "Jewish Survival" in *Light from Jewish Lamps, A Modern Treasury of Jewish Thoughts*. Editor, Sidney Greenberg. Northvale, NJ: Jason Aronson, Inc., 1986.

Weitzmann, Chaim. In *The Jewish Anthology*. Editor, Edmund Fleg, translated by Maurice Samuel. New York: Behrman House, 1933.

Wiesel, Elie."A Plea for the Dead" in *Legends of our Time*. New York: Holt, Rinehart and Winston, 1968.

—In *Voices from the Holocaust*. Editor, Sylvia Rothschild. New York: New American Library, 1981.

—*Night/Dawn/Day*, originally published as *Night/Dawn/The Accident* by Hill and Wang, a division of Farrer, Straus, Giroux, 1972.

—In *The Jewish Woman in Contemporary Society*. Editor, Adrienne Baker. New York: New York University Press, 1993.

Whitehead, Alfred North. "An Appeal to Sanity," in *Atlantic Monthly, vol. 163*.

Wilson, Woodrow. *Public Papers of Woodrow Wilson, vol. II*. New York: Harper and Brothers, 1925.

Wise, Stephen. In *Light from Jewish Lamps, A Modern Treasury of Jewish Thoughts*. Editor, Sidney Greenberg. Northvale, NJ: Jason Aronson, Inc., 1986.

—In *American Jewish Album—1654 to the Present*. Editor, Allon Schoener. New York: Rizzoli International, 1983.

Wouk, Herman. *This Is My God*. Boston: Little Brown, 1987.

Yezierska, Anzia. *Children of Loneliness*. New York: Funk and Wagnalls, 1923.

Zangwill, Israel. In *A Book of Jewish Thoughts*. Editor, Joseph Herman Hertz. New York: Bloch Publishers, 1954.

Zimmerman, Bonnie. In *People of the Book: Thirty Scholars Reflect on Their Jewish Identity*. Editors, Jeffrey Rubin-Dorsky and Shelly Fisher-Fishkin. University of Wisconsin Press, 1996.

Zola, Emile. "J'Accuse!" in *L'aurore*, 13 January 1898.

PRAYER BOOKS

ArtScroll: Weekday Siddur. Editors, Nosson Scherman and Meir Zlotowitz. Brooklyn, NY: Mesorah Pub., 1990.

Gates of Prayer: for Shabbat and Weekdays. Editor, Chaim Stern. New York: Central Conference of American Rabbis, 1994.

Gates of Forgiveness. Editor, Chaim Stern. New York: Central Conference of American Rabbis, 1980.

Gates of Repentance: Mahzor for the High Holidays. Editor, Chaim Stern. New York: Central Conference of American Rabbis, 1978.

Gates of Mitzvah: A Guide to the Jewish Life Cycle. Editor, Simeon J. Maslin. New York: Central Conference of American Rabbis, 1979.

The New Light Siddur. Editor, Barry Friedman. New Jersey: Temple B'Nai Abraham, 1991.

The Union Prayerbook for Jewish Worship. Cincinnati: Central Conference of American Rabbis, 1947.

Permissions

The editor wishes to acknowledge with sincere gratitude the permission granted by the publishers and authors to print the following material:

To Be a Jew

Jack Reimer. *Wrestling with the Angels*. Jack Reimer, editor. Copyright © 1995 by Jack Reimer. Reprinted by permission of Schocken Books, a division of Random House, Inc.

Bonnie Zimmerman. In *People of the Book: Thirty Scholars Reflect on Their Jewish Identity*. Edited by Jeffery Rubin-Dorsky and Shelly Fisher-Fishkin. University of Wisconsin Press: Madison, Wisconsin, 1996.

Edmund Fleg. "I Am a Jew" in *Why I Am a Jew*, translated by Louise Waterman Wise, Block Publishing Co., New York, 1929. Reprinted by permission of Ayer Company, Publishers.

Alicia Ostriker. In *People of the Book: Thirty Scholars Reflect on Their Jewish Identity*. Edited by Jeffery Rubin-Dorsky and Shelly Fisher-Fishkin. University of Wisconsin Press: Madison, Wisconsin, 1996.

Letty Cottin Pogrebin. "Confessions of a Contradictory Jew." Copyright © 1998 by Letty Cottin Pogrebin. Originally published in *National Council of Jewish Women Journal*. Spring 1998.

I. B. Singer in *Dialogues in Judaism: Jewish Dilemmas Defined, Debated, and Explored* by Rabbi William Berkowitz. Reprinted by permission of the publisher, Jason Aronson, Inc., Northvale, NJ © 1991.

Alexander M. Schindler. From the Presidential Address to the Union of American Hebrew Congregations, December 2, 1995. Reprinted by permission of the author.

Leo Jung, "Between Man and Man" in *The New Treasury of Judaism*, third ed., 1977, by Philip Birnbaum, published by Hebrew Publishing Company. Reprinted by permission of the publishers.

It's a Tradition!

Anne Roiphe. Reprinted by permission of Simon & Schuster from *Generation Without Memory* by Anne Roiphe. Copyright © 1981 by Anne Roiphe.

Leo Baeck. *The Essence of Judaism* by Leo Baeck. Copyright 1961 by Leo Baeck. Reprinted by permission of Schocken Books, a division of Random House, Inc.

Sandy Sasso Eisenberg, "Pledge to Our Adopted Child" in *A Ceremonies Sampler.* Edited by Elizabeth Resnick Levine; Woman's Institute for Continuing Jewish Education, La Jolla, California. Reprinted by permission from the author.

David Cohen. The *Jews in America.* David Cohen, editor. Copyright © 1989 by Collins Publishers, Inc. Reprinted by permission of HarperCollins Publishers, Inc.

Gates of Prayer: The New Union Prayerbook. © 1975 Central Conference of American Rabbis, and used by permission.

Jonathan Rosen. *The Talmud and the Internet: A Journey Between Worlds.* Copyright © 2000 by Jonathan Rosen. Reprinted by permission of Farrar, Straus and Giroux L.L.C.

Sandy Eisenberg Sasso, excerpt from *Putting God on the Guest List.* Copyright © 1996 Rabbi Jeffrey K. Salkin. Reprinted by permission of Jewish Lights Publishing, P.O. Box 237, Woodstock, VT 05091.

Jeffreyn Salkin. *Putting God on the Guest List.* Copyright © 1996 Rabbi Jeffrey K. Salkin. Reprinted by permission of Jewish Lights Publishing, P.O. Box 237, Woodstock, VT 05091.

"Sunrise, Sunset" by Sheldon Harnick and Jerry Bock © 1964-Alley Music Corp. and Trio Music Co., Inc. Copyright renewed and assigned to Mayerling Productions, Ltd., and Jerry Bock Enterprises for the United States and to Alley Music Corp., Trio Music Co., Inc. and Jerry Bock Enterprises for the world outside the United States. Reprinted by Permission. All rights reserved.

Robert Eisenberg. *Boychicks in the Hood—Travels in the Hasidic Underground* by Robert Eisenberg. Copyright © 1995 by Robert Eisenberg. Reprinted by permission of HarperCollins Publishers, Inc.

Barry Friedman. From "Wedding Ceremony." Reprinted by permission of the author.

Anita Diamant. *Living a Jewish Life* by Anita Diamant and Howard Cooper. Copyright © 1991 by Anita Diamant and Howard Cooper. Reprinted by permission of HarperCollins Publishers, Inc.

Paula Reimers, "Mikveh Journal," in *Lechem Tafayl: The Student Journal of the Jewish Theological Seminary;* Winter 1990. Reprinted by permission of the author.

Gates of Mitzvah: A Guide to the Jewish Life Cycle. Edited by Simon Maslin. Copyright © 1979 Central Conference of American Rabbis. Reprinted by permission.

Ari Goldman. *The Search for God at Harvard* by Ari L. Goldman. Copyright 1991 by Ari L. Goldman. Used by permission of Times Books, a division of Random House, Inc. Permission for Canadian rights graciously granted by Markel Enterprises, Inc, New York.

Philip Roth. Reprinted by permission of Simon & Schuster from *Patrimony* by Philip Roth. Copyright © 1991 by Philip Roth.

Jack Reimer. *Wrestling with the Angels.* Edited by Jack Reimer. Copyright © 1995 by Jack Reimer. Reprinted by permission of Schocken Books, a division of Random House, Inc.

Patricia Z Barry. In *Wrestling with the Angels.* Edited by Jack Reimer. Copyright © 1995 by Jack Reimer. Reprinted by permission of Schocken Books, a division of Random House, Inc.

Yehuda Amachi. "On My Father's Memorial Day," in *Amen* by Yehuda Amichai. Copyright © 1977 by Yehuda Amichai. Reprinted by permission of HarperCollins Publishers, Inc.

The Jewish Yearbook—5657 (1896). Edited by Stephen W. Massil and Anne J. Kershen. Reprinted by permission of the publisher, Vallentine Mitchell & Co., Ltd.

Alfred Kazin. Excerpts from *A Walker in the City*, copyright 1951 and renewed 1979 by Alfred Kazin. Reprinted by permission of Harcourt, Inc.

Emanuel Rackman, "Can We Moderns Keep the Sabbath?" in *Commentary*, September, 1954. Reprinted by permission.

Sue Levi Elwell, "Rosh Hashanah Sermon, September 24, 1987," in *Four Centuries of Women's Spirituality*. Edited by Ellen M. Umansky and Dianne Ashton (Beacon, 1992). Reprinted by permission of the author.

Letty Cottin Pogrebin. Crown Publishing Group for permission to quote from *Deborah, Golda and Me* by Letty Cottin Pogrebin. Copyright © 1991 Letty Cottin Pogrebin.

David Cohen. *The Jews in America* by David Cohen, Editor. Copyright © 1989 by Collins Publishers, Inc. Reprinted by permission of HarperCollins Publishers, Inc.

Herman Wouk. *This is My God*, Little Brown and Company. Copyright © 1959 by The Abe Wouk Foundation, Inc. Copyright © renewed 1987 by Herman Wouk. Reprinted by permission of the BSW literary agency.

COMING TO AMERICA

Emil Hirsch. A *Book of Jewish Thoughts*. Edited by Joseph Herman Hertz. Bloch Publishers: New York, 1954. Reprinted with permission.

Maurice Samuel. *The World of Sholem Alechem*. Alfred A. Knopf. Copyright © 1944 by Maurice Samuel. Reprinted by permission of Alfred A. Knopf, a division of Random House.

Irving Howe. *World of Our Fathers*. Copyright © 1976 by Irving Howe. Reprinted by permission of Harcourt, Inc.

Marcus Ravage. Excerpt from *World of Our Fathers*. Copyright © 1976 by Irving Howe. Reprinted by permission of Harcourt, Inc.

Alexander Harkavy. *American Jewish Album: 1654 to the Present*. Edited by Allon Schoener. Reprinted by permission of Rizzoli International. Copyright © 1983.

Morris Raphael Cohen. *A Dreamer's Journey*. Beacon Press, 1949. Reprinted by permission of Ayer Company, Publishers.

Abba Hillel Silver. "America." Reprinted by permission of Adele Silver.

Anna Novotney in *Jews of America* by Francis Butwin. Behrman House: New Jersey, 1969/1973. Reprinted by permission of Behrman House.

Sydney Stahl Weinberg. *World of Our Mothers*. Copyright © University of North Carolina Press, 1988. Reprinted by permission.

Rachel Mittlestein in *World of Our Mothers* by Sydney Stahl Weinberg. Copyright © University of North Carolina Press, 1988

Israel Davidson in *Out of Endless Yearnings: A Memoir of Israel Davidson*; by C. Davidson. Bloch Publishers: New York, 1946. Reprinted by permission.

The Jewish Yearbook—5657 (1896). Edited by Stephen W. Massil and Anne J. Kershen. Reprinted by permission of the publisher, Vallentine Mitchell & Co., Ltd.

David Cohen. The *Jews in America*. David Cohen, Editor. Copyright © 1989 by Collins Publishers, Inc. Reprinted by permission of HarperCollins Publishers, Inc.

Philip Roth. Excerpt from *The Facts: A Novelist's Autobiography* by Philip Roth. Copyright © 1988 by Philip Roth. Reprinted by permission of Farrar, Strauss and Giroux, L.L.C.

Chaim Potok in *Jewish Wisdom* by Rabbi Joseph Telushkin. Copyright © 1994 by Rabbi Joseph Telushkin. Reprinted by permission of Chaim Potok.

Philip Roth. Excerpt from *The Facts: A Novelist's Autobiography* by Philip Roth. Copyright © 1988 by Philip Roth. Reprinted by permission of Farrar, Strauss and Giroux, L.L.C.

Paul Cowan. *An Orphan In History: Retrieving a Jewish Legacy*. Doubleday, 1982. Reprinted by permission of Rachel Cowan.

Chaim Potok in *The Jews in America* by David Cohen, Editor. Copyright © 1989 by Collins Publishers, Inc. Reprinted by permission of HarperCollins Publishers, Inc., and of Chaim Potok.

WE REMEMBER THE SIX MILLION

Judith Miller. *One by One by One: Facing the Holocaust*. Simon and Schuster, © 1990 by Judith Miller. Reprinted by permission of the author.

Alexander M. Schindler. "God and the Holocaust," from Holocaust Commemorative Program, College of the Holy Cross, April 7, 1999. Reprinted by permission of the author.

The New Light Siddur. Written and edited by Barry Friedman. Copyright © 1991 Temple B'nai Abraham, Livingston, New Jersey.

Lucjan Dobroszcki. *Chronicles of the Lodz Ghetto, 1941–1944*. Edited by Lucian Dobroszycki, translated by Richard Lourie. New Haven: Yale University Press, 1984. Reprinted by permission.

Jan Mawult in *In the Warsaw Ghetto: Summer, 1941*. Willy Georg, Rafael F. Scharf, Aperture Foundation, Inc., New York, 1993. Reprinted by permission.

Mary Berg from *In the Warsaw Ghetto: Summer, 1941*. Willy Georg, Rafael F. Scharf, Aperture Foundation, Inc., New York, 1993.

Hillel Seidman. In *Blessed is the Daughter*. Meyer Waxman. Shengold Books, a division of Schreiber Publishing, Rockville, MD, 1999. Reprinted by permission.

Petr Fischl, "Terezin" in *I Never Saw Another Butterfly: Children's Drawings and Poems from Terezin Concentration Camp 1942–1944*. Reprinted by permission of the Jewish Museum in Prague.

Miroslav Kosek. "It all Depends on How You Look at It" in *I Never Saw Another Butterfly* U.S. Holocaust Memorial Museum. Edited by Hana Volavkova. Copyright 1978, 1993 by Artia, Prague. Compilation © 1993 by Schocken Books. Reprinted by permission of Schocken Books, a division of Random House, Inc.

Pavel Friedmann. "The Butterfly" In *I Never Saw Another Butterfly* by U.S. Holocaust Memorial Museum. Edited by Hana Volavkova. Copyright 1978, 1993 by Artia, Prague. Compilation © 1993 by Schocken Books. Reprinted by permission of Schocken Books, a division of Random House, Inc.

Toward the Land of Milk and Honey

The New Light Siddur. Written and edited by Barry Friedman. Copyright © 1991 Temple B'nai Abraham, Livingston, New Jersey. Reprinted by permission.

Yehuda Amichai. *Poems of Jerusalem* by Yehuda Amichai. Copyright © 1988 Yehuda Amichai. Reprinted by permission of HarperCollins Publishers, Inc.

Schlomit Grossberg. In *My Shalom, My Peace: Paintings and Poems by Jewish and Arab Children.* Edited by Jacob Zim and Uriel Ofek. Copyright 1975. Reprinted by permission of the McGraw-Hill Companies.

Gassoub Serhan. In *My Shalom, My Peace: Paintings and Poems by Jewish and Arab Children.* Edited by Jacob Zim and Uriel Ofek. Copyright 1975. Reprinted by permission of the McGraw-Hill Companies.

Amichai Yehuda. *Poems of Jerusalem* by Yehuda Amichai. Copyright 1988 © Yehuda Amichai. Reprinted by permission of HarperCollins Publishers, Inc.

Marc Chagall. "Speech made at the dedication of the Chagall Windows of Hadassah Medical Center, Jerusalem, 1962." Reprinted by permission of Hadassah, the Women's Zionist Organization of America, Inc.

Golda Meir. *My Life* by Golda Meir. Copyright © 1975 by Golda Meir. Reprinted by permission of Putnam Berkley, a division of Penguin Putnam, Inc. Canadian publisher Weidenfeld & Nicholson.

Rachel Ogen. In *Testament: At the Creation of the State of Israel.* Edited by Aaron Levin. Artisan: New York, 1998. Reprinted by permission of the author.

Barry Friedman. "Eitan Gissen Memorial Service." Reprinted by permission of the Author.

Saul Bellow. *To Jerusalem and Back, A Personal Account.* Viking Press: New York, 1976. Reprinted by permission.

"Shir La' Shalom" (A Song of Peace)—Lyrics: Yahacob Rotblit. Copyright © by author—ACUM Israel. Reprinted by permission.

As Others See Us

Oswald Garrison. Excerpt from *Fighting Years: Memoirs of a Liberal Editor.* Copyright 1939 by Oswald Garrison Villard and renewed 1966 by Henry H. Villard and Oswald G. Villard, Jr. Reprinted by permission of Harcourt, Inc.

Dmitri Shostakovich. *Testimony, The Memoirs of Dmitri Shostakovich* as related to and edited by Solomon E. Volkov. English language translation

PATHS OF PRAYER

WORDS OF WISDOM

ABOUT THE AUTHOR

INA ABRAMS is a journalist and (under the name Ina Yalof) the author of four books on medical issues, including *Open Heart Surgery: A Guidebook for Patients and Families; Life and Death: The Story of a Hospital* and *Straight from the Heart: Letters of Hope and Inspiration From Survivors of Breast Cancer*. She has published many articles in magazines and newspapers. This is her first book on Judaism.

She lives in New York with her husband.